Aussie Stories

Aussie Stories

Over 40 Inspirational Stories by:
BARRY CHANT · KARL FAASE
MICHAEL FROST · CHRISTINE CAINE · GORDON MOYES
KEL RICHARDS · SHERIDAN VOYSEY
AND MANY MANY MORE

STRAND PUBLISHING
Sydney

First published 2009 by Oasis Publishing.

ISBN 978 1 921202 02 5

Distributed in Australia by:
KI Entertainment
Unit 31, 317–321 Woodpark Rd
Smithfield NSW 2164 Australia
Phone: (02) 9604 3600
Fax: (02) 9604 3699
Email: sales@kientertainment.com.au
Web: www.kientertainment.com.au

Cover photography courtesy of Ken Duncan Australia Wide Pty Ltd (www.kenduncan.com). Copyright © Ken Duncan.

Edited by David Dixon
Copyedited by Owen Salter
Cover design by Joy Lankshear
Typeset by Midland Typesetters, Australia
Printed by McPhersons Printing Group

Contents

Aussie Stories

Looking Back

Grenville Kent

~

Backing the Camry out of the garage, I heard a baby's voice screaming and felt my wheels crunching little bones. I braked too late and ran to the back of the car, and there was Marcus, our sixteen-month-old, crushed and dying in blood.

Then I woke in fright.

I looked around the dark bedroom at my calmly sleeping wife, the digital clock redly glowing 3:19 am. I slowed my breathing and silently asked God to care for my family, then turned over; if I didn't sleep, my congregation might during my sermon later that morning.

I woke up late, quickly prayed, reread the sermon over breakfast, dressed and sprinted to the car, ready to back it out and load the children while Carla prepared the truckload of bottles and baby gear.

Sitting with the car in reverse and the handbrake off felt like a familiar scene—and I remembered my dream. But I had locked

Marcus into the dining room twenty seconds before. I checked the mirrors and looked out the back window. Nothing. Still I sat there arguing with myself, my foot on the brake. Maybe my dream was from God, maybe mere parental fear. I looked at my watch in frustration—then got out of the car anyway.

There behind the back offside wheel was my little boy. He was playing with Bear and his red car. He saw me and shouted excitedly, 'Dadda! Car! Car!'

I scooped him up for a hug, though he wasn't the one who needed it.

How on earth did he get there? Through a closed internal door, across the lounge-room, out through the locked front door and screen door, across the stone porch with its uneven surface and then down to a crawl to duck under the opening Roll-a-Door without me seeing him. I didn't know he was capable of that Houdini routine, let alone in under half a minute.

I clipped him into his seat with a rather mechanical thanks to God, seated his sister and backed the car out. When his mother joined us, I told her what had nearly happened. I was emotionally numb—the classic male coping mechanism. I told my church about it, and they gasped, but I still felt like I was telling someone else's story from a book.

I don't see miracles every day. I want a faith that is rational, not the flipped-out 'God sends me messages in my tea leaves' variety. Don't get me wrong; I believe that God can 'break' natural laws—the Bible describes miracles, and I've seen a few. I believe that God still acts and intervenes, but that most of God's gifts arrive quietly through natural systems the Creator originally set up. So I thank God for food even though it doesn't fall from the sky like manna.

With Marcus, though, I couldn't find a natural explanation. My subconscious could have just popped up that dream, I guess—but on that night? What are the chances?

I can only conclude it was a miracle. Call it a minor suburban miracle, but it shows me beyond reasonable doubt there is a God who sees the future and loves my son. My mind was convinced, and that afternoon my heart finally caught up in a Kleenex moment of relief and gratitude.

Yet miracles are slippery things. They raise as many questions as they answer. Why us, in a world where so many children suffer? We have praying friends who have suffered terribly with a child dying young or, perhaps even worse, growing up to live a destructive and tragic life. How do I tell this story to them? How did God choose when to intervene? And what if God had not chosen to do a miracle that day? Would I still trust?

Miracles don't remove all doubt. You can eat loaves and fishes and see healings—and still walk away from the Teacher. You can eat manna and enjoy shade from a cloud that follows you around day and night—and stay lost in rebellion against prophetic leadership. When people demanded miraculous signs before believing, Jesus refused, saying that the only sign they would see would be his teaching and his death (see Matthew 12:38–40; John 6:30–36).

The gospel may be the only sign you ever get. Paul observed that in his day 'Jews demand miraculous signs, and Greeks demand their "wisdom", but we preach Christ crucified—a scandal to the Jews and nonsense to the Greeks; but to those who are called (both Jews and Greeks), the cross shows Christ as the power of God and the wisdom of God' (1 Corinthians 1:22–24, paraphrased).

The gospel is sign enough. God's greatest intervention in history was his own Son crushed and dying in blood (Isaiah 53:10).

I won't let my inability to explain theodicy in the entire universe stop me from enjoying God's clear interventions, or from trusting God's kind omniscience. Or from loving the gospel that saves me and my family at such savage cost to the Father's Son, his other Self. Unthinkable love! 'God did not keep back his own Son, but allowed him to die for us all. After that, wouldn't any other gift be mere small change?' (Romans 8:32, paraphrased).

The Climb

Jane Beale

The weekend away had a dual purpose: first, to spend some much-needed time with myself; second, to be far enough away that I could *not* pick up my daughter from a sleepover at her Dad's place. It had seemed the right thing to do in the past—responding to my daughter's late night requests to come home. By continuing to step in, however, I knew I would limit her opportunity to develop a relationship with her father.

As hard as it was, I had decided to get right out of the way—250 kilometres away.

My budget accommodation was a small, basic cabin in a seaside tourist park. Once unpacked, I drove into town and treated myself to a meal at a fancy restaurant. Rather than having my spirits lifted, I felt alone and vulnerable. Sitting there eating, on my own, I found myself dwelling on the fact that I was thirty-eight, divorced and had no one special in my life to accompany me on a weekend away.

Solemnly, I returned to my cabin. I tried numerous locations around the tourist park but there was absolutely no reception on my mobile phone. Trying to convince myself that my daughter and I would both survive without our planned good night call, I went to bed.

It was a long night of fitful sleep and distressing dreams. Every time I drifted off, my daughter was there, calling out to me, but I couldn't reach her. When the first rays of sunlight appeared, I felt exhausted.

After breakfast, I decided to climb 'The Bluff'. I would stroll along the southern beach until I reached the turn off to the stony inland pathway. Then I would make the climb up to the lookout point. My reward would be stunning views of the bay and the surrounding townships. I couldn't wait to see it!

I set off at a good pace, water bottle in hand. Once I reached the end of the sand, I looked back towards the tourist park and calculated that I'd come more than a kilometre. Somehow I'd missed the entrance to the path. Rather than turn back, I thought that if I just kept going, I would eventually reach the tip of the peninsula and could climb up to the lookout from there.

The shoreline was rocky as I continued on but the unevenness of the surface did not deter me. Nor did the look of concern from a solitary fisherman who acknowledged my passing.

A check of my watch showed I'd been walking for nearly an hour, so I sat down to rest my legs. I felt God quietly speaking to my heart, but I chose not to listen, preferring instead to watch a group of sailing boats heading out to sea. Some were beginning to raise their sails and I could just make out the crews shouting orders to each other.

Had I turned my attention inward, I might have heard God saying: 'Turn back—it's not safe.' Or perhaps I might have heard: 'Keep going—I am with you.'

Screwing the lid back on my now half-empty bottle of water, I noticed the terrain ahead consisted of a series of narrow, rocky ledges. I struggled along for a few minutes but soon had to concede that the cliff face was becoming impassable.

My focus turned to a rising annoyance at the possibility of having to go back. A lapse in concentration and suddenly I was slipping. Grabbing a piece of rock that jutted out in front of me, I managed to steady myself, but the sound of my water bottle bouncing down the rocks sent a chilling message. *Be careful!*

Looking down to see how far the bottle had fallen, I wondered whether it was worth retrieving.

'Get the water!' resounded clearly in my head.

Muttering under my breath, yet trusting this inner wisdom, I started the frustrating descent to the bottom of the cliff.

After recovering my bottle and the ground I'd lost, I searched for a way to continue on. I caught a glimpse of blue sky through a gap in the rock. The narrow tunnel ahead of me was just high enough to slide through on my stomach, but too deep to see through to the other side.

Returning to the tourist park back along the beach now seemed the most sensible course of action. I was a mother. Recklessness was a luxury I had given up years ago.

Glad I'd been blessed with a sense of caution, I stepped away from the hole. Then, as if compelled by some unknown force, I turned back and wriggled through.

Standing on a new rocky ledge, I felt euphoric at having made it to the other side. Looking around at my new location, I couldn't make out where I was in relation to the lookout point. In fact, I couldn't see the top of the landmass above me. I realised the Bluff was much bigger than I'd first anticipated.

With no obvious way forward, I just stood there, taking in the smell of salt air and the freshness of the wind. A check of my watch showed it was eleven o'clock. Two hours had passed since I'd first set out. I had expected to be back enjoying a cup of tea by now. I took a sip of water then carefully replaced the lid. I was going to have to make what little I had left last.

I set my sights on the next ledge and began manoeuvring towards it. I kept this up, clambering inelegantly from one ledge to another, until the inevitable happened—I became stuck.

Trying to carrying on forwards, I realised there was nothing to grab hold of. I tried to go back but my feet, now unsteady with fatigue, slipped each time I tried to secure a foothold. Despite repeated attempts, I was not able to move from my current position.

Thoughts of needing assistance came to mind—complete

with images of my rescuers shaking their heads at such stupidity.

Why had I been so determined to go on? Retracing my steps had seemed so unsatisfactory. Now, meandering safely back along the flat, sandy beach was highly appealing!

Calling out to God for help seemed a pathetic thing to do. I had knowingly got myself into this situation—why should I now expect him to get me out of it?

I knew it would most likely be ages before anyone even realised I was missing. I could be stuck out here for hours, dehydrating and falling victim to exposure.

I wondered about the fisherman. Would he alert the authorities that he'd seen a woman venturing a long way out onto the peninsula? It was a slim hope, but it was all I had. I was certain no one else had seen me.

With no food and little water, it was going to be a long, uncomfortable wait. I *could* take the risk and try again to climb back to the previous ledge. Maybe then I could make it back to the tunnel and the beach. But what if I slipped and fell? I could be lying out here all night. Alone . . . injured . . . or worse.

I lowered myself into the best sitting position I could manage. I stayed that way, cramped and uncomfortable, for a long time. Eyes closed, hugging my knees to my chest, I thought about my brave little girl. I was like her now—wanting the comfort of a mother's loving arms.

I contemplated the times I had encouraged others to find

their inner strength while leading performances with my signing group—*The Singing Hands Choir.* A recent experience with the much-loved song 'You Raise Me Up' came to mind.

With hands uplifted, basking in God's loving grace, I'd watched with amazement as the words to this inspirational song penetrated deeply into the souls of the people standing before me. As many hearts opened, we had celebrated together God's ability to raise us up to be so much more than our limited, human selves.

Drawing strength from this memory, I found myself humming the notes of the song. Before long, I realised I was singing it out aloud: 'You raise me up . . .' I was on God's shoulders now, no longer feeling small and helpless. Sure-footed and growing in determination, I saw myself conquering the Bluff by climbing up onto the trees.

Eager to turn vision into reality, I looked up to see a sturdy branch hanging down over the rock, from the top of the cliff face. At full stretch, I could just clasp it with my fingertips. In a leap of faith, I jumped up, grabbed it and hung on for dear life.

I stepped my feet slowly up the rock, digging my shoes in hard wherever I could find a foothold. The tree limb swayed under the load. Shifting first one hand, then one foot, I steadily pulled myself up. The muscles in my arms and shoulders were burning from supporting my full weight, but I didn't stop. I kept climbing until my body was fully up on the branch.

Once up, I found the tree difficult to negotiate. Trying hard to block out the discomfort of sharp twigs poking into my skin, I pushed my way through the thick foliage onto the internal limbs. I knew I needed to take my time in order to distribute my weight evenly across the flimsier branches. One false move and I felt sure a branch could snap and drop me back over the edge of the cliff.

With a face-full of scratches and a hair-full of tree matter, I finally reached the base of the trunk and was able to put my feet onto earth. Flat, solid ground had never felt so good.

What followed was a long, exhausting fight through dense scrub. Just when I thought I could go no further, the land began to clear. Walking more freely, I picked up the pace and there it was—the stony pathway! It had taken four hours along the most treacherous route, but I had finally found it!

Mustering my remaining strength, I turned and set out along the path. But I didn't turn left back towards the tourist park. I deliberately turned right and headed upwards, towards the lookout point. I'd set out to climb the Bluff and that was what I was going to do, even if it took every last bit of my strength.

It was an exhausted and battered body that finally made it back to the tourist park in the middle of the afternoon. Weak with hunger, I staggered into my cabin and collapsed onto the bed. My feet throbbed, my legs ached and my chaffed hands were scratched and sore. However, the pain in my physical body was overshadowed by a sense of spiritual well-being. I had reconnected with my inner strength and was glowing with a renewed enthusiasm for the precious gift of life.

Later that night, a change in atmospheric conditions brought with it a pleasant surprise. With three bars of reception showing on my mobile phone, a call came in from my daughter. Excitedly, she informed me she had tried surfing for the first time. I could tell she was thriving and was undoubtingly finding her *own* inner strength.

'I miss you so much, Mummy,' she said sincerely, 'but I'm so proud of myself for sleeping at Dad's. I'm not even so scared about tonight now, 'cause I know I can do it!'

My little girl was okay. We were both okay, having survived and grown through our separate experiences. There would be so much to talk about as we shared our stories about the challenges and accomplishments of this significant weekend.

Ironically, the view from the lookout at the top of the Bluff had not been spectacular. Overgrown trees had all but blocked out any sight of the bay. Having taken so many steps to finally reach the summit, it was not the outcome I had strived for.

Far from feeling disappointed, I was able to reflect on the immense spiritual rewards of the climb. I'd experienced firsthand that life really isn't all about the destination. It is the transformation that takes place within us as we venture along the journey that makes it worthwhile.

Ultimately, when we humble ourselves and draw on our inner strength—*God's strength within us*—we can climb any mountain and weather any storm.

The Charlotte Rocker

Gordon Moyes

~

$\mathcal{M}$ost of Australia's regional airports are pretty good. I have flown into almost every one of them. Some, like Albury, Dubbo, Tamworth, the Alice, Cairns, Port Augusta, Burnie and Esperance, are as good as anywhere in the world. Newcastle is my favourite and it has been judged the best regional airport in Australia.

The regional hub airports in the USA are beyond anything we can imagine. With the US population and its affluence that allows so many to fly so frequently, you would expect it. Many of their regional airports are bigger than those in Sydney or Melbourne. Then there are huge airports like LAX, SFO, O'Hare and JFK. At Atlanta you need to take a train to various terminals! Every time we've arrived in Atlanta, we've been on our connecting flight before our luggage has been, so that it has to be home-delivered the next day.

But the regional hub I enjoy most is the one I fly into every time I go to the US: Charlotte, South Carolina. We pick up a commuter aeroplane there to take us to Johnson City where I teach at the Emmanuel School of Religion. Charlotte is the last word in Southern hospitality to be found in an airport.

Charlotte Douglas International Airport is more than a major hub for air traffic. It is a destination with activities to keep air travellers entertained during layovers. Apart from excellent shopping, dining and other services, the airport provides a unique way of helping you pass the time while you're waiting. Along all the windows of the airport are hundreds of white rocking chairs.

These casual, country-style rockers are found throughout the South in living rooms, near the hearth, and on the front porches of houses and farms. They have carefully crafted back slats, curved arm rests and a carved seat. They are highly ornamented with turned oak spindles, and are much higher in the back than other rockers, providing a head rest.

Crafted from North Carolina oak, they were introduced to the Charlotte airport in 1997 as part of a photography exhibit. Now, sprinkled throughout the airport, they invite weary travellers to rock the time away and enjoy a bit of the Southern lifestyle.

That means you can be served a beer while you are rocking, or a barbecue pork sandwich with the smoky, vinegar-based sauce with the slight tangy bite that people in the South enjoy. You can have a manicure and a pedicure to melt away the stress of air travel. If you enjoy the experience enough, you can even buy a rocker and take it with you—for just $US900!

The free rock in a Charlotte rocking chair gave me the idea of making one for our wide verandah back in Australia. Then I discovered they were for sale at every Cracker Barrel Old Country Store. There is a chain of over 550 Old Country Stores across the US, each combining a retail store and a restaurant that serves traditional Southern comfort food. The front porch of a Cracker Barrel store has rows of white Charlotte rocking chairs for guests to enjoy before or after eating, and there is usually a fireplace and a checkers table in the dining area for an added country feel. The store carries mainly nostalgic merchandise, collectibles, old time toys, classic candies, scented candles and recordings of old radio programs. And, of course, you can buy your own rocking chair for only $US200, flat packed and ready to go.

My hankering for a Charlotte rocker was part desire, part hope, part prayer, part plan. But whether at $900 or $200 they were too expensive for me.

Then I visited a woodworking shop and was able to buy a set of plans to make my own. This project sat in the back of my mind for four years or so. One summer holidays I finally wanted to start, but my set of plans had somehow been misplaced or thrown out when we'd moved house. I felt thwarted.

At a garage sale a few months later I saw a smaller white rocker for sale. I took it home to sit on our back porch. It wasn't a Charlotte, but it would have to do.

Then while I was driving home one night, my car headlights

shone on a pile of rubbish at the side of the road waiting for the council pick up. As I passed I saw, sticking up in the air, what looked like some spindles from the back of a rocking chair. I backed up and, sure enough, they were spindles, long, thin and beautifully turned.

The turning was going to be the most difficult part of making my own. Any woodworker will tell you that long, thin spindles are very demanding to turn on a lathe. The American Shakers knew how, but modern furniture makers know how hard it is.

Among the rest of the rubbish I found two curved arms, and the bow rockers and their struts, the rungs, the cross rails and the legs. All the pieces were there. I thought of taking them home just for kindling for the fire until I saw the seat. It was hand carved and solid, and I knew I had to do something with it.

But everything was in pieces. I realised that this rocking chair had been left out in the weather, and the rain had caused all the wood joints to come apart.

Later in my workshop I laid out all the parts. I took a shaving of wood to identify it as the weather had removed all of the paint. It was oak. That meant it was unlikely to have been made in Australia, and it certainly wasn't one of those cheap pine rockers sold in our shops. Because it was oak it had not split in the rain. The long spindles indicated it was a very large rocker. And then in the seat, in the holes for the spindles, I discovered something else—little wedges of wood. That rocking chair had been made with invisible joints, not just glued together and held by screws or nails. This was a serious bit of fine furniture, ruined by being left in the rain.

I sanded all the pieces and started putting them together like a one-and-a-half metre high jigsaw. I made some more little wedges and then started to clamp and glue the whole thing. I've always said a woodworker can never have too many clamps, and now I had every one I possessed, plus strap clamps and even long floorboard clamps, all compressing the chair together. I let it dry for a week, and then the big test. It rocked away without a hint of complaint.

It was only when it was all together that I could see that this big rocker was a Charlotte rocker. No doubt about it. It was an oak Charlotte rocker, made in the USA. How did it come to Australia? Did some migrating American family bring it over in a container of their belongings? And who would put such a fine piece of furniture out in the rain?

By the time I'd finished, it had been reassembled, sanded, glued and painted with two coats of undercoat and a top coat of white enamel. Now it is sitting on our back porch looking at the bush. And God provided it for free.

We have our desires, our plans, our hopes and our prayers. But God often answers before we can do anything about them.

The Bearded-Lady Jesus

Michael Frost and Alan Hirsch

In the early 1850s, William Holman Hunt, one of the founders of the avant-garde Pre-Raphaelite movement, painted an immeasurably popular picture, *The Light of the World*. In this image, Jesus is standing outside a closed, heavy, wooden door, under a stone archway. He gently raps on the door with the back of his open hand. In his other hand he holds a jewel-encrusted lantern. The scene is dark, and behind him can be seen wild woods with twisted branches silhouetted against the setting sun. It seems that Jesus has braved an inhospitable terrain to make it to this ivy-covered door.

Hunt said, 'I painted the picture with what I thought, unworthy though I was, to be by Divine command, and not simply as a good subject.' The picture is certainly reminiscent of the text of Revelation 3:20: 'I am standing at the door, knocking; if you hear my voice and open the door, I will come in to you and eat with you, and you with me.'

It's hard to quantify the popularity of this image. At the

turn of the twentieth century, it toured Canada, Australia, New Zealand and South Africa and was seen by thousands. In Australia more than five hundred thousand people saw it in Sydney and Melbourne in a time when the combined populations of those cities was fewer than a million people. Across the United Kingdom, postcard-sized copies were made, and people couldn't get enough of them. They carried the image like a keepsake or a relic. Servicemen were given copies to keep in their uniforms, a physical reminder of the closeness of Jesus to them in their time of battle. The Salvation Army composer, Sir Dean Goffin, was inspired by the painting to compose his most famous piece, also entitled *The Light of the World*. Hunt's original is now in a side room off the large chapel at Keble College, Oxford, and he painted a large copy toward the end of his life, which is now in London's St Paul's Cathedral.

A closer examination of Hunt's Jesus reveals some interesting observations. For example, the wooden door has no exterior handle. It can obviously only be opened from the inside, adding weight to its portrayal of the passage from Revelation 3. Furthermore, Jesus is somewhat feminised. He is wearing a silk ball gown (we're not sure what else you'd call it) and a royal red robe or cape. He has a golden crown on his head, flattening his glorious blond, shoulder-length hair. His beard is blond, too, and his serene gaze makes him look more like a mythic English king than a Middle Eastern radical. In his genuine attempt to portray Jesus' kingly grandeur, Hunt has cast him as King

Arthur or Richard the Lionheart perhaps, a wise, unruffled, beautiful English monarch. A classic co-option.

We call it the bearded-lady Jesus. Flowing blond locks swept back from the face, high cheekbones, groomed eyebrows, full lips, with heavenward-gazing, gentle eyes—he's beautiful. But is this a valid biblical representation of Jesus? Or is this a mere fantasy object for an overly sentimental, cultural Christianity? This is the inoffensive Messiah, clean and tidy, pleasing to the eye. This is no disturber of our souls. This image of Jesus reflects a spirituality that is anchored in an adoration of the wonderful Christ, the unattainable Jesus.

A few years back, when Michael was teaching a seminar to Salvation Army officers in New Zealand, he noticed that most of the members of the audience were wearing black T-shirts with the revolutionary slogan 'I'll fight' emblazoned in red across the back. This was an allusion to a famous sermon by the Salvation Army founder, William Booth, who claimed that while there was poverty, alcoholism and suffering on the streets of London, he'd fight it with all his might. It's a dramatic and motivational slogan. But hanging on the wall in the seminar room, dominating the whole space, was the picture of Jesus shown above. Michael pointed this out and asked whether the Jesus depicted in that painting would ever fight against anything, let alone get down into the filthy alleys and laneways of nineteenth-century London to serve the poor. One officer present admitted that the bearded-lady Jesus probably informed their Christology far more than the example of William Booth, a holy warrior if ever there was one.

The bearded lady in these paintings exudes an abstracted serenity, gentleness and peace. And yet the Jesus we meet in the Gospels is at times frustrated, disappointed, annoyed and, worse still, angered. He is full of holy pathos. He exasperated his rivals, unsettled his friends and drove his enemies mad. Says Alison Morgan, 'Jesus was a difficult and uncooperative revolutionary who so threatened the established order of the day that there seemed to be no option but to have him executed.'

The Bible quotation is from the New Revised Standard Version.

Smileys from God?

Nicole Startling

~~~~~~~

My son Jacob's school has an elaborate awards system. His teacher also uses as a form of discipline in the classroom, the 'name on the whiteboard' technique. If you are being especially good, your name goes up on the smiley side of the whiteboard. If you are misbehaving, you go on the side with the sad face. Then there's a system of ticks and crosses . . . you get the picture.

Well, yesterday Jacob came home and told us he got on the smiley side. It's not *that* unusual that he did, but this time we were really pleased when he told us the reason. It was because he had comforted one of the other boys when he had got upset about losing a game. We talked about it for a while, and then he told us that he had actually told the teacher about his actions. As it happened, she said she had already noticed, but we felt we should tell him that he didn't need to tell the teacher whenever he did the right thing!

After we had explained that it really only mattered that God saw his actions, Jacob thought about it for a little while and then said: 'All right, next time that happens, I won't tell the teacher, I'll just *imagine* that I'm getting a smiley from God.'

So here's the issue. Once, I think, I would have felt profoundly uncomfortable with language like this. I was taught to recoil with horror at the idea of getting 'brownie points' from God. And of course there is something correct that was being guarded in this reaction—we don't even begin to 'earn' anything from God, as if we were good enough for him to owe us something.

But lately I've been thinking that in all that contempt for the 'brownie points' mentality I was ignoring a big, big theme of Jesus' teaching, and the teaching of the rest of the Bible. I never want my kids to think that they can earn their way to heaven, but as sinners saved by God's grace, I do want them to live to please him, and to delight in doing the things that make God's face smile.

So we didn't trash Jacob's idea of the divine 'smiley faces'— though we did translate the language into an encouragement to think about God seeing and smiling. (Is that different? it feels a tiny bit different to me!) And now we pray that he does remember that, and that it becomes more and more the motivation of his heart.

From the Ashes of Black Saturday

Adele Nash

~

It was eerily silent on the property between Buxton and Narbethong, Victoria, where the Bird family—David, Lorna, and children, Stephen, 11, and Sarah, 7—had lived in their modest home for three years. Now, it was just a pile of twisted metal, ash and a few scorched items that survived the 7 February 2009 bushfire.

They were but one family among thousands affected by the bushfires that devastated dozens of towns and settlements across Victoria on that black Saturday.

A multitude of crows broke the silence as they flew over, calling to each other dismally, their sleek black feathers blending into the landscape of the quiet valley. Everything around was black.

As I walked with David and Lorna around the site where their house once stood, David paused and said, 'Look, you can see the remains of our Bibles.'

He bent down to leaf through the pages but they dissolved into ash that scattered in the breeze. Yet despite losing everything but their two cars, the members of the Bird family, with a strong Bible-based faith, were counting their blessings.

On 7 February, with temperatures rising into the high 40s and the wind strengthening, the fire danger was great. But life continued as normal that morning. The family, being members of the Seventh-day Adventist Church, had left early on Saturday morning to attend church in Healesville. Lorna was on duty as a volunteer at a nearby health centre, where David worked as a lifestyle consultant.

After church, along with the children, he joined her for lunch. Following lunch, the family took some of the centre's guests to Lake Mountain, east along the road that runs through Marysville, where David hoped it would be cooler.

'In fact, it was,' he told me. 'But I got a call at 3.30 pm saying there was smoke on the range. When it began to happen, we were still up at Lake Mountain. I was uneasy because I had guests with me. I had to get them down the mountain as fast as I could. We raced back to Marysville. I felt quite relieved when we got there—we were back in civilisation.'

David said Marysville was quite normal at the time, which was around 4.30 pm. No one was panicking, there were no emergency vehicles and people were shopping.

However, a large cloud of smoke loomed to the north.

'We went back to the health centre, arriving about 4.45, and that's when we saw the big cloud come thundering toward us,' said David. 'It was like a line of volcanoes. It sounded like thunder.'

By 7.30 that night, the smoke was so thick around the centre it was as if the sun had set. By then they couldn't leave. It was only the arrival of a westerly wind shift that saved them and the others sheltering at the centre, as the fires wiped out the hamlet of Narbethong a couple of kilometres to the east.

Others would not be so fortunate, with heavy loss of life just fifteen minutes away. The Birds lost neighbours who had stayed to defend their property.

As the Birds drove to their property late the next day, they prepared themselves for the worst. Along the road, they passed cars in which they knew people had died. There were also many dead animals along the way.

David said, 'When we were going through Narbethong and Marysville, we realised it was bad. We talked to Stephen and Sarah beforehand but we weren't sure how they'd take it. We felt it would be best for them to be involved from the beginning, but it was launching into the unknown.

'At this stage, we didn't know our neighbours had been killed. The children knew their guinea pigs were gone, but they also knew we weren't as seriously affected as others who had lost relatives.'

When they arrived at their home, said Stephen, he didn't want to get out of the family car. 'I saw the pile of corrugated iron that had been the roof of our home. But the important thing is we're still alive and still have Jesus in our hearts.'

But how easy is it to keep Jesus in your heart and see hope at a time like this?

'I think there are always things we can be thankful for,' David told me, 'but one thing that's struck me is that if we look for hope, we will find it. We know that God understands and suffers, too.

'When we look to Christ and his life and death and resurrection, we see suffering there. To me, that's where the answers are found—that God understands and suffers. Also, he offers us hope and says that suffering will not go on forever. I find that the most satisfying approach.

'One day, we'll understand everything. But for me, now, I can see there is hope, though our lives are shattered in various ways. And there are symbols of that hope.'

Such symbols, he said, include chickens hatching at the home of a friend and seeing green shoots springing in their vegetable plot, even though there had been no rain.

'Nature hasn't given up, God hasn't given up and neither should we,' said David stoically.

However, people will ask where God was during the unfolding tragedy, and how he could stand by and allow it to happen.

In response, David said, 'The question of suffering is probably the biggest question in life. My opinion is that there really is no adequate, intellectual answer. There's an emotional answer that meets our need, and that's found in knowing God is all-powerful but also suffers with us. Why innocent people and children die is really a heartbreaking mystery, but I don't think it should be something to make us doubt God's love.'

Love, support and care from friends and family were vital for the Birds during this time. Even small things helped. One such small thing was among a bag of toiletries given to Lorna by a friend. It contained a tiny torch and a pack of tissues. Said Lorna, 'When we had to break the news to our son that our neighbours had passed away, we all sat on the bed and cried together. As I reached for those tissues, I thought of her kindness.'

Even in the midst of the devastation the Birds were looking to the future. They planned to be part of the renewal of the community and continue working in the area. 'We know a lot of people in Marysville, and the community feels the right thing to do is rebuild and keep the community spirit alive,' said David. 'I want to be involved in that.'

A disaster helps people to evaluate their priorities. And from the Christian's perspective, said David, 'realising we're pilgrims passing through the valley of tears but with the hope of a better future reminds us God and his promises are always there.'

'We have realised how much more important family and friends are than our possessions,' said Lorna. 'The loss of the house isn't something we've mourned over too much. But the way we're getting through this is by God sustaining us and by the prayers of people.'

The Difference a Night Can Make

Karl Faase

❧

*I*f you had met Ron Baker early in the mid 1950s you would have wondered about the possibility of a positive future for him or his family. Ron was an illiterate, hard living Australian bloke. He was a bus driver who spent many of his evenings drinking and was abusive to his wife, Beryl. His early years had not given him a good start in life and now he was struggling to make a go of it as a husband and father.

I met Ron in 2008 while making a documentary of the 1959 meetings in Australia of American evangelist Billy Graham. Graham and his team were in Australia between February and May 1959. Over those four months more than 3.25 million people attended crusade meetings in Australia and New Zealand, 25 per cent of the then population. The final rallies in Melbourne and Sydney were estimated at 143,000 and 150,000 respectively. The crowd in Sydney was so large that organisers had to run simultaneous meetings at the Sydney

Cricket Ground and the Sydney Showground to cater for all those who wanted to hear Billy Graham speak. Over this whole period, 130,000 Australians, or 1.24 per cent of the population, responded to Graham's call to follow Jesus, and the very fabric of Australian society was influenced.

When I interviewed Ron I spoke with a fine gentleman who is now a father, grandfather, ordained Baptist minister and well-known speaker. Ron's whole life is marked by being committed to his family and seeking to share Christian faith with other people.

What made the difference in the life of Ron Baker? It was one surprising evening early in 1959.

As a bus driver, Ron had been out to the Billy Graham meetings at the Sydney Showground several times. He never went in and was annoyed by the whole process. Ron was especially aggravated because his wife had attended one night and ended up out the front, praying with a counsellor in the pouring rain. When she arrived home soaking wet and dripping on the family's new carpet, Ron lost it.

A few nights later Ron had the opportunity to swap out of a driving shift and so avoid making the trek out to the Showground. Instead of going out drinking, which was his usual practice on evenings off, he went straight home. When he got there he was met by a builder mate who literally begged Ron to go to the Graham crusade that night. Ron couldn't believe it when he gave in and went. His one night of not having to go to these annoying crusades and he is on his way to the Showground again. He sat at the back, negative and uninterested.

At the end of his meetings, Billy Graham would invite people to make a choice to follow Jesus. As an indication of this decision, he asked people to get out of their seats and walk to the front. Ron had no intention of taking up religion, and to this day he doesn't know how he got to the front with the thousands of others who responded that night. All he knows is that when he was asked why he was there, he said he wanted to become a Christian using language and terms that the counsellor had probably not heard before at a crusade meeting.

That evening was the start of a radical change in Ron's life. Over the course of the next several years he learnt to read, went to college and studied the Bible, and became an ordained Baptist minister. Ever since he has given himself to following Jesus and sharing how his life had been changed by God.

The final scenes of the *Remembering '59* documentary are of Ron and Beryl Baker sharing a meal with their two children and five grandchildren. Ron's son is a senior pastor of a regional Baptist church and his daughter is a counsellor in pastoral care at her local church, helping young women and their families. His grandchildren are seeking to follow Jesus. Here is the picture of the difference faith in God can make.

Where would Ron Baker be today if his life had not been changed by Jesus? Ron himself doubts that he would even be alive. This story is not just a testimony to the remarkable 1959 Graham Crusades; it is a testimony to the power of God to change an individual.

How Long?

Anusha Atukorala

~⌒~

I loved it. I loved the music that resonated all around the busy shopping mall. A musician was hard at work, playing his heart out. I stopped, enchanted; I listened. Hearing the soothing melodies made me feel good inside, so light and airy and joyful. I walked over and had a look at the CDs. Should I buy one? It would be our wedding anniversary in a week's time. Perhaps it could be part of my anniversary gift for my husband of twenty-three years.

I mused for awhile. *Yes*, I decided, *I'll go for it!* I stepped forward.

The musician looked delighted when I asked to purchase a CD. 'Of course!' he said. I asked him which of the many albums displayed he'd recommend. He chose one and gave it to me. 'This has music from popular films and is a favourite. It's the one I sell the most,' he said.

I told him it would be a gift to my husband for our wedding anniversary the next weekend. But I don't think he heard me.

He was too busy trying to sell his wares. He gave it to me, adding, 'Put it on today when you have dinner. You'll enjoy it!' I almost opened my mouth to speak, to reiterate what I'd already told him, that it was a gift and would not be played till the next weekend. But then, I knew there was no point. He wasn't really concerned about what I wanted to say. He was just happy to make another sale.

I placed his CD in my bag and started moving away. As I pushed my trolley along the shopping mall, I recalled another little encounter that had occurred just before. That was very different.

I had bought a few groceries. While I was paying for my purchases, the salesperson chatted to me. He was a nice young lad—a Year 11 student. As he checked out my groceries, he thoughtfully asked if I'd like to take the card I'd bought in my hand, rather than have it placed in the bag of groceries with the risk of its being crushed. I readily agreed and took it from him.

As I pulled out the cash to pay him, he asked me, 'How long?' I looked at him puzzled. *How long?* Whatever did he mean? He saw my confused expression and grinned. 'How long have you been married?' And then it struck me. The card I'd purchased was an anniversary card for my husband. It had actually been placed inside the envelope, so the lad must have seen what it was when he took it out briefly to scan the bar code.

I was impressed by his perceptiveness. 'Oh,' I said with a

smile. 'Twenty-three years!' As I left the shop I was still smiling, surprised not only at how this young man noticed the card but that he cared enough to ask how long I'd been married.

The two encounters that day with two strangers taught me something about myself. How often am I interested in other people? I like to think I am deeply interested in their well-being. But am I? Really?

Am I like that young lad who was perceptive and caring enough to ask a question that made me smile? Or am I so busy doing what I have to do—like the gifted musician—that I actually miss something important that someone wants to tell me? And would I care enough to ask again if I didn't hear, rather than discount it altogether?

In Their Shoes

Aaron Hardke

C omfortable shoes. In preparing for my expedition to Nepal, I knew comfortable hiking shoes were essential. I did my homework. I read about shoes. I studied catalogues. I examined pictures. I talked about shoes. I explored the pros and cons of various materials and compounds. I knew what to look for. I was ready to purchase. Then I tried some on—*hhhhmm, not quite what I expected*. Then another pair—*I don't think so*. A third pair—*Aaaahhh, perfect*.

Nothing could prepare me for a walk in those comfy boots. No photos, no catalogue, no technical specifications, no sales pitch. Nothing conveyed the reality of the comfort I experienced when my foot slipped into those boots. Walking in shoes is the only way to know what they are *really* like.

When my $270 super-comfy, light-weight, waterproof hiking boots first touched the dirt floor inside the mud-brick and bamboo classroom at Beldangi II Refugee Camp in eastern Nepal, I wondered if my little backpack loaded with pencils and

36

pads would make a difference to the 45,000 Bhutanese refugee children in the camps. I wondered if a few kilos of gifts I had packed were a fair trade for the immeasurable gifts the refugees gave me—the gifts of courage, hope and humility. I doubted it. The gift of awareness I received will certainly outlast the shiny pencils and clean paper I left in Nepal.

My pencils may not have changed their lives, but the pen of the Bhutanese Government certainly did. That pen signed the Bhutanese Citizenship Act in 1985, leading to the expulsion of ethnic, religious and linguistic minority groups in an attempt to maintain national identity. By the late 1980s, 125,000 Bhutanese people, almost 20 per cent of the entire Kingdom's population, had been forcibly removed by the Bhutanese Government, the vast majority finding refuge in eastern Nepal. The United Nations High Commissioner for Refugees (UNHCR), with the support of other aid agencies, established the camps in Nepal as a response to the crisis.

Together with seventeen other teachers from Lutheran schools across Australia, I set out to experience firsthand the work of Lutheran World Federation Nepal, supported by Australian Lutheran World Services (ALWS). The teacher study tour, organised by ALWS, revealed the reality of the displaced and underprivileged. Visiting six refugee camps, numerous schools, children's homes and empowerment programs ensured that I had the opportunity to walk in the shoes of others. I was no longer simply reading, studying or flicking through brochures—I was experiencing the reality: the sights, sounds, tastes, smells, temperatures, textures, emotions. I was living.

The two-week tour took us through a sensory wonderland of crowded refugee camps, each with its own school staffed by untrained and under-resourced teachers. An average of approximately forty-five students packed into small, simple bamboo shelters. No windows, no electricity; just a mat, book and pencil for each student. Meanwhile, their teachers made use of a small old blackboard and a single stick of chalk. The fruits of their labour were astonishing; students were in many cases achieving higher than non-refugees in Nepal. This was especially evident in their level of spoken English. The students studied diligently, despite the insecurity of their future, despite the state of their classrooms. Your options are limited when your whole life and foreseeable future are contained within the boundaries of a camp. Homeless. Jobless. Uncertainty.

Despite the despair and uncertainty, there is an overwhelming sense of pride in the camps. The bamboo huts are well maintained (except the one that was destroyed by a passing elephant just hours before our visit). Students, staff and camp leaders shared many stories; they shared their passion, their heartbreak, their frustration. They shared their hopes and dreams: 'Don't give us fish, help us get a river and we will catch our own fish.' Tears landed on my shoes as I tried to imagine standing in theirs.

We heard personal stories about forced 'voluntary migration', about desires for repatriation or resettlement, about going to bed hungry when there isn't enough sun to cook your rice rations in the solar oven. Yet among the appalling conditions and heartbreaking stories, we witnessed hope. Students who imagined, teachers who dreamed and camp leaders who inspired. Imagine filling their shoes.

We were surrounded by despair, destruction and pain. Yet God was everywhere. We saw him work through the volunteers who support, maintain and advocate for the camps. They weren't preaching the gospel messages of love and service; they were living them. We witnessed his wonderful creations: the majestic Himalayas and the gifted refugee children who painted in the foothills of the towering giants. We felt his hand as our feet walked through the camps. We are truly blessed by him.

We left Australia hoping to learn about the refugee crisis. We returned with more lessons about ourselves. We had dreams of providing life-changing gifts to the refugees. Instead, our lives were changed. I wanted to help the refugees, but God used them to help me. Through their lives, God taught me about my life. We gained a new appreciation for our own gifts from God and our own lives—blessings we take for granted. But not anymore.

Prior to the study tour, we had done our homework. We researched the Bhutanese camps. We read about refugees. We viewed pictures. We studied the statistics. We talked about refugees. We listened to stories. Nothing, however, could have prepared us for the experience when we stepped into the refugee camps, the schools and homes of the severely underprivileged. Nothing conveyed the reality we faced when we walked through the camps. We may not have taken an extended walk in their shoes, but we certainly tried them on—shoes they have been wearing for seventeen years. We experienced the conditions; we felt the passion, the frustration, the determination. We experienced firsthand a snapshot of life in these camps.

I thought I knew about injustice, about courage, about service. I thought I had an appreciation of the gifts God has so richly blessed me with. I had done my homework. But just like selecting the right hiking boots, I learnt that you can only *really* know if you take a walk in someone else's shoes.

With God as My GPS

Barry Chant

~

For my birthday last year, my family gave me a Global Positioning System receiver—otherwise known as a GPS.

A few days later, I needed to drive right across Sydney. It was the ideal opportunity to try it out. It was not an auspicious start. In fact, I think I nearly gave the young woman who operates it a heart attack.

I wondered what her name was. GPS . . . Gloria Priscilla Sharon? No, too flowery. Gertrude Prudence Sophia? Nup, too old-fashioned. Genevieve Panchalea Savannah? Mm, that was more like it. Daring, oriental, wild. Genevieve had a motoring tradition about it. The middle name had a hint of panache. It had once been the name of an Indian princess. But Savannah was the one I liked—with its echoes of fresh air and blue skies and sweeping grasslands. I could picture her dancing and skipping through the open spaces, laughing and singing with joie de vivre, her flared skirt swirling around her—an image, alas, that was not particularly consistent with being trapped inside a small black box affixed to the windscreen of a car. Geneva Prudence Selena? Mm, possibly. Serious, efficient, with echoes of law-making, sagacity and caution. And appropriate for a progressive young woman executive who might well enjoy directing traffic and telling people where to go. So Geneva it was.

I had a general idea of my destination. So when Geneva spoke to me the first time, I guessed which route she had in mind—and it would involve the M5 motorway. But it was Friday evening, and if I ventured on to the M5 I knew there was every possibility I would finish up sitting stationary for a long time in a huge traffic jam, while the snarling, panting vehicles banked up for their usual weekend unhappy hour. So I chose another longer but quicker route for the first part of the journey.

Geneva was not happy.

'Turn left at Sylvania Road,' she ordered, adopting a royal tone that didn't suit her. I ignored her. She was obviously a bit taken aback by my apparent inability to understand a simple instruction. So she became more specific. 'In 150 metres, turn left,' she commanded me. Again I ignored her.

'Turn left, turn left!' she cried, now growing increasingly annoyed.

I disregarded her again and entered the Princes Highway. She was now noticeably disturbed. I continued to disobey and she became confused. 'Turn right at Acacia Road,' she demanded.

Now I knew she was panicking. You could only turn left at Acacia Road. The right turn had been blocked off for years. I drove smugly past. 'Sorry, sweetheart,' I said, apologetically. 'Can't be done.'

She began to sulk. I don't think she was impressed with being called 'sweetheart' by someone she had only met for the first time that day. Especially someone who couldn't comprehend simple directions in plain English. But she guided me carefully past Bangor and Menai until I reached Heathcote Road, although she was obviously doing it grudgingly.

'Stay on this road for ten kilometres,' she remarked coldly. It was almost a threat. I imagined that if I could see her eyes they would be either black or steel-blue, the kind that a ruthless princess might have, the kind that showed little mercy for disloyal subjects. But maybe underneath that apparent officiousness, there was a soft heart. I tried to picture her with warm green eyes, tinged with pity for one so wilful as I. Maybe there was even a touch of fear that I might do myself serious harm if I wasn't more observant. But after she refused to speak to me for the next quarter of an hour I knew I was right the first time. Definitely black or steel-blue.

I turned on to the Hume Highway and then to the M7. I could almost hear Geneva's sigh of relief. I still wasn't following the original route but she could now see that if I listened to her carefully there was a remote chance I would still finish up at the right place. She waited in silence, without a word. But

I knew she was watching me closely every metre of the way. She didn't trust me now and still suspected I might do something else unpredictable.

'Stay on this route for the next 30 kilometres,' she said slowly, so that I couldn't possibly misunderstand. At the same time, the GPS screen seemed brighter. She obviously wanted to show me where I was as well. I imagined her operating some kind of hidden control panel to achieve this helpful outcome. Or was it just the fading sunlight that made the screen easier to read?

I drove on happily for nearly half an hour and began to wonder if Geneva wasn't a bit like God. When we need directions he's right there to give them. If we take a wrong turn, he tells us how to get back on track. And I wondered if I was not rather too much like me. So confident in my own ability and too ready to treat God like a lowly assistant to be called on for help only if needed.

By the time I'd sorted out the theological implications of all this, the Richmond Road exit came into view and I slowed down. Geneva became alarmed, evidently fearful that I was about to leave the motorway too soon. I knew she had her hand over her eyes and I could picture her shoulders slumped in despair at my incompetence. There were signs of an ominous 'oh no!' in her tone as she warned me to keep going. To her obvious surprise, I obeyed her. I could almost see the look of relief in those steel-blue eyes.

'Had you worried that time, Ginny,' I said, half to myself. But she heard me. 'Ginny?' I fancied her muttering with annoyance. 'Ginny? Who said you could call me Ginny?' She directed me stiffly to take the next exit. I was sure she was wrong but decided to do so anyway, just in case. After a short distance I mumbled to myself, 'Mm, Ginny was right after all.' I'm sure I heard her whisper, 'I told you so.'

'Take the second exit from the roundabout,' she instructed. I counted carefully and took the third. I pictured her shaking her head and sighing with resignation. I am sure the GPS, stuck firmly as it was to the windscreen, moved marginally and mournfully from side to side.

'Do a U-turn as soon as possible,' she cried with a note of impatience in her voice. And in case I missed the message, she said it again.

'Don't worry, Geneva,' I told her. 'I'll turn at the roundabout. Keep your socks on.'

I swept around the traffic island and headed back in the right direction. She seemed gratified and patiently explained which corner to take next. I obeyed without protest, as I did humbly at the next two intersections as well.

With all this last-minute meekness and docility, I thought I had won her heart, but when I arrived at my destination, she flatly refused to speak to me any more.

I didn't need her help to get home and left her packed away safely out of the sight of vandals.

I still didn't know if we were on speaking terms or not. But my wife Vanessa took her out the other day and they seemed to get on all right.

I decided that the next day I would try again. Maybe if I smiled nicely when I set her up she would be more amiable. All I had to do then was turn her on.

And meanwhile, I'll still keep working on that crucial question. If God is my GPS, how much do I listen? Hopefully, at the end of the journey, with all my wrong turns and false exits, I will still find myself arriving safely at those long-awaited Golden Gates.

The Postie's Mate

Margo Mangan

~∂~

We were travelling from Tamworth to Sydney. Like thousands of Tamworth residents, we chose to stop at the Aberdeen Pie Shop on the way. It's less than two hours down the highway, but no matter what time we set out during the day, Aberdeen always seems to be the perfect time to break our journey, and the pie shop becomes the perfect place to stop, stretch, and 'refuel' our bodies. The tiny shop has the best range of pies, sausage rolls and cakes along the New England highway. Often there's quite a line of trucks pulled up level with the pie shop, in mute testament to its widespread popularity.

As we began to cross the busy highway we noticed a postie's motorbike parked outside the shop. Nothing unusual in that— pie shop owners *do* get mail. As we reached the footpath we noticed there was a cockatoo sitting on the bike's handlebars ... on a specially constructed perch. The cocky wasn't tethered to the perch but was simply sitting on it in the sunshine. He was wearing an Australia Post tag attached to one of his feathers.

47

Interesting!

As we made our way into the pie shop, the postie was exiting. We made our selections, paid for them and moved out. The postie, the bike and the cocky were still outside the shop as we emerged. The postie was happily sharing his pie with the cocky, who seemed to be relishing the pastry. He held it with one claw as he attacked it with his beak.

We spent a few minutes chatting with the postie while he continued to share his meal with the cocky. He filled us in on their daily routine. The cocky went to work early each morning with the postie, hanging around while he sorted the mail. He then accompanied the postie on his route around the town. The cocky had the opportunity to fly off into the nearby bush if he wanted to, but seemed perfectly happy to travel around on his perch on the handlebars of the bike.

The postie obviously enjoyed the company of his cocky as he went through his daily routine. The cocky also enjoyed the company of his owner, and preferred that lifestyle to the freedom of life in the wild. Both delighted in each other's company.

At its best, my relationship with God is a bit like the relationship between the cocky and his owner. God and I choose to hang out together, enjoying each other's company. We share little moments, like a meal, the beauty of a flower, or time in the warm sunshine on a chilly winter's day. Sometimes I'm as aware of God as the postie is aware of his cocky, perched on the handlebars in front of him. That's when my life seems fulfilling, satisfying and enjoyable.

At other times I lose focus and forget that God is there with me, ready to share my day. That's when life becomes less than satisfying, and feels frustrating and hollow.

God isn't visible to me in the way that the cocky is to the postie—I guess that's one of the reasons why I sometimes forget he's there. But his presence is just as real, and our enjoyment of each other's company is just as special. And just as the cocky has never chosen to take off and desert his postie friend, I know that God will never desert me.

Is God Necessary?

Sheridan Voysey

~

A couple of years back, *New York Times* columnist Maureen Dowd visited Australia to promote her book *Are Men Necessary?* At one Sydney event, Dowd and an interviewer stepped on stage, took their seats and settled in to discuss their topic. Soon into the conversation, though, a voice from the audience asked if a podium blocking the view could be moved. Before the interviewer could get up from her chair, two men leapt from the front row and on to the stage. The men heaved aside the heavy podium emblazoned with the words, 'Are Men Necessary?' The audience broke into laughter as the interviewer quipped, 'I think the question has been answered.'

In recent years a handful of loud voices have proclaimed the wonders of atheism, the irrationality of belief and the nonsense of matters divine. In their own words, authors like Richard Dawkins, Christopher Hitchens and Sam Harris have posed the question: 'Is God Necessary?' As I ponder Maureen Dowd's experience, I wonder if there's an ironic twist here. As the armchair debates take place, could God already be on the stage answering the question by his very actions?

'Is God necessary?' the critic asks—when his very words are spoken with breath that God has given him (Genesis 2:7).

'There is no God,' says the atheist—as she bathes in the sunshine and drinks up the rain that God provides (Matthew 5:45).

'I'm living fine without God,' says the humanist—unaware that his birth place was determined by God (Acts 17:26) and that every hair on his head has been counted (Matthew 10:30).

'God is the cause of all evil,' some say—and yet we benefit from hospitals, aged-care homes and charities all created in the name of God.

'God is a crutch for the emotionally weak,' others claim—and yet it was God who inspired William Wilberforce, Martin Luther King Jr, and other reformers who fought slavery and racism, and outlawed things like infanticide and gladiatorial combat.

'God is dead,' wrote Nietzsche—and yet how many times has that God leapt onto the stage when we've been in a personal spot of bother?

Many years ago two men were walking along a dusty road, talking about religious matters. As they walked, a third person joined them. They didn't recognise the face, but the words of their fellow traveller set their hearts beating. They urged him to stay a little longer, and then over dinner their eyes were miraculously opened. The stranger turned out to be Jesus.

51

The swag of nouveau atheistic books released in recent years is stimulating discussion, and for that I'm most glad. But wouldn't it be ironic if, as we debated the existence of God, he turned out to be walking right beside us? Wouldn't it be ironic if he were already on the stage helping out?

May our eyes be opened.

Catch the Right Train

Christine Caine

A few years ago, my husband, Nick, and I walked through an unexpected and very challenging experience. We found out we were pregnant with our second baby, and we were ecstatic. We were having the time of our lives being Mummy and Daddy to Princess Catherine, and all three of us were very excited to meet this new addition to our family. We waited as long as we could control ourselves to tell our friends all over the world, but once we opened the floodgate, the news spread very quickly. It seemed as if neither Nick nor I could go anywhere without being stopped and congratulated. We were so excited that so many people were enthusiastic about our pregnancy.

Then one day I went with a friend to a routine doctor's appointment. The doctor began to listen for the baby's heartbeat, which I was very excited to hear for the first time. I held my breath and listened intently for the rapid, miraculous sound of the tiny life inside of me. The doctor seemed to be taking a long time to find it, and by the look on his face I knew that something was seriously wrong. After several minutes, he said the words no expectant woman wants to hear: 'Christine, I'm so sorry, but I can't find a heartbeat.'

I could never have imagined that a routine appointment might turn so dark and that my great expectations would turn into my greatest fear. My automatic response was denial. I urged the doctor to get a new monitor, because clearly the one he was using was broken. Instead, he scheduled an emergency ultrasound that confirmed that the small life inside of me had died.

To say I was utterly shocked is an understatement, and at that instant my mind was bombarded with so many destructive trains of thought. Sitting on the platform of my mind, just waiting to depart with me on them, were thoughts of guilt. I wondered, *Is this my fault? Have I caused this to happen because I didn't slow down my travelling schedule?* Also on the platform were thoughts of fear: *Is this because I'm almost forty? Are all those grim post-thirty-five pregnancy statistics really true?* And thoughts of doubt: *Did I lack the faith that might have prevented this tragedy? How does this fit with my faith in God's providence?*

In addition, the trains of depression, discouragement, failure and isolation were calling for me to board. These would have inevitably taken me to a destination from which it would have been very hard to return.

It was in this moment of great grief and pain that the

strength of my mind muscle was going to be tested. Would I still believe that God is good, even when my circumstances were not? Would I be able to trust him, even though I could not understand why this had happened to me? Was I willing to apply the truth of the Word to this situation despite the disappointment?

My emotions were screaming on the inside. Although the sense of loss and overwhelming sadness I felt was very real, I had to choose to set my mind on things above. The only way that I was going to get through this was by choosing to set my mind on God's eternal Word rather than my current circumstance. I clung to Psalm 23:4: 'Yea, though I walk through the valley of the shadow of death, I will fear no evil; for You are with me; Your rod and Your staff, they comfort me', and Psalm 46:1: 'God is our refuge and strength, a very present help in trouble.'

In the days following my loss, I also took care to be constantly in the house of God. At times my mind muscle was not strong enough to carry the weight of my sadness and I needed to be surrounded by people who would help me to stay on track. I had to be in an environment in which positive trains of thought were constantly passing by the platform of my mind. Eventually, I would jump on one.

It was during one of these worship services that we sang the song 'Blessed Be Your Name' by Matt Redman. The lines, 'Blessed be Your name on the road marked with suffering, though there's pain in the offering, blessed be Your name' were just words to me one week earlier, but now they had become my heart's cry. This song articulated everything that I felt, while keeping me on the right track.

I had that song on repeat in my car, my iPod—just about anywhere I could play music. The words were easy to sing when everything was going well in my life; the challenge was to keep blessing the Lord in my darkest hour. By choosing to magnify God in the midst of my difficult circumstances, I was making him bigger than the pain I felt.

It was during one of these times of worship that I had what can only be described as a supernatural encounter with God in which he healed my heart. I can't explain it in any other way, but in those moments God did what months of counselling could not have accomplished. He took my grief and filled me with a renewed hope for my future. He truly turned my mourning into dancing and my sorrow into joy. I believe this happened because I had made a choice to take on his thoughts and his ways in the midst of my challenges and adversity. It's only during times of trials that the true strength of our mind muscle is revealed. What is in us will always flow out of us during these times.

I wanted to share this deeply personal story with you to encourage you that no matter what circumstances you might be facing right now, it is possible for you to overcome in the midst of them by taking hold of God's thoughts. It may not always be the easiest thing to do, but trust me: if I can do it, you can do it, too. The same Holy Spirit who helped me strengthen my mind muscle is also there for you, no matter who you are or what your past looks like.

Bible quotations are from the New King James Version.

I Hear Voices

Ian Stoltz

Hi, my name is Ian. I'm thirty-seven, 195cm tall, and I enjoy music and movies. I don't tend to read books very much but I do play guitar. I like to have a beer or, ahem, four. I love spending time with my friends and family. I like to play squash. Oh, and also—I hear voices . . .

Imagine a little waterfall flowing onto the back of your head. Lovely and relaxing. After a while, though, your neck gets a bit stiff, so you move. But imagine if that sensation stays there, no matter how much you move your head, or even if you get up and walk away. It's always there; you can't escape from it.

At the same time there is a pesky fly buzzing around your head. It stays on the edge of your field of vision. It doesn't make any noise, but it has a kind of gravitational pull on your mind that catches your attention and pulls at your thoughts.

But there's more. Even when you are alone you can hear people talking. You can't quite make out what they are saying, but you do know that for some reason they always seem to be talking about you.

With the waterfall and the fly, and the people talking about you, you would probably have trouble concentrating when you were reading a book or listening to someone speaking. Actually, having a normal conversation would be almost impossible.

Oh yes, add one more thing—the feeling that your brain is slowly rotting. It feels like cells inside your head are popping, like bubbles would in a glass of beer. Welcome to my world.

Well, it used to be my world. That description will give you an idea of what it was like for me when I was diagnosed with schizophrenia back in January 1995, when I was almost twenty-three. My family had noticed my erratic behaviour and booked me in to see a psychiatrist. It was not difficult for them to see that something was wrong with me. I would scream at empty air. I would walk from inside the house to outside and back again, over and over. I hardly ate, and my personal hygiene wasn't that good. One morning I smashed my $400 acoustic guitar. Pretty unusual behaviour for a quiet, shy kid from the country.

It was a strange experience for me having to tell someone what was going on inside my head. After I had finished, my psychiatrist said, 'Well, it's obvious you have [a slight pause] schizophrenia.' Followed by a polite nod.

My first thought was, 'So, that's what schizophrenia is.' Often a person suffering from mental illness is the last to know.

To give you a classic definition, a schizophrenic is a person who suffers from visual or aural hallucinations—seeing people or hearing voices, for example. The term 'schizophrenia' is used to describe a range of irregular mental processes in the brain, in some cases cellular changes and even damage in areas of the brain. We don't really know what causes it, but we're able to treat it with a greater degree of success than ever before.

After my diagnosis I had to struggle, in the real sense of the word. My illness would have completely overtaken my ability to function if I hadn't. I would most likely have died, one way or another. So I struggled to survive, literally.

I was raised as a Christian in a strict Lutheran family. My dad died when I was nine years old. I started smoking cigarettes when I was fifteen, and a year later I started drinking beer on the river bank on Friday nights with some other kids my age. It was just a tough, country-boy thing to do. I was trying to fit in, mainly because I was the one who always got teased at school.

In 1992, when I was almost twenty, I was accepted into university to study computer science. That's when I first tried marijuana. I flunked my first year at uni, not because of the marijuana but because of this amazing thing called 'email'. I missed many lectures because I was spending so much time sitting in computer-terminal rooms chatting to my friends via email.

In late 1993 I tried LSD for the first time. It was about four or five months after this that I began to hear 'people' talking in the background somewhere. My initial reaction was that someone had a camera and was spying on me. I thought it was a prank.

A couple of days went by and I just couldn't get my prank theory to make sense. It might have, except for one factor: How did they know what I was thinking? I was getting pretty confused. I smoked pot to 'calm' myself. It's funny how we can lie to ourselves so easily.

Over the next few weeks I thought that someone, somewhere in the world, must have developed the ability of mental telepathy—like in science fiction. It must have been a worldwide event of opening every mind. A few months after that I remember thinking it might have something to do with the part in Revelation where it says 'the books were opened' (20:12).

This is where things started to get really bad for me. When you believe that your thoughts are no longer private, every bad thing you have done becomes public knowledge. I believed that people could see everything I had ever done wrong because they had access to my thoughts. Imagine how you would feel if every single thing you had ever done wrong became public knowledge.

For months on end I felt terrible, more terrible than I had ever felt before. As time went on, the feeling became so bad that I felt as though my body was starting to break down and my mind was shutting down. It felt like I was rotting inside.

Schizophrenics often suffer from various delusions, and I was no exception. I remember sitting at a friend's house one evening, not long after I first started getting symptoms, and I was watching *Hey, Hey, It's Saturday*. It seemed to me as if this was a special episode. I wasn't sure why. But suddenly this mental telepathy thing was happening through the TV. I could talk to Daryl and Ozzie in my mind and they would react to what I was thinking. This 'ability' extended on to other TV shows, and later I believed that I could communicate via the radio and even through recorded music and old movies.

Not long before this, Jesus and the angels had come to talk to me. Don't get excited; this was just another delusion. How do I know? Because Jesus was doing stuff that Jesus doesn't do. He was telling me that he could trick me, for example, and I knew that Jesus doesn't do that. The angels were doing some strange stuff, too. They had a mass of rules—things like 'Memory isn't allowed, learning isn't allowed, getting your thoughts in the wrong order isn't allowed, farting isn't allowed.'

Among it all I also believed that I knew how the beast, the 'small horn' mentioned in Daniel 8:9, was going to cut off the holy people. I knew this because there was a telepathic TV camera mentally attached to the back of my head which could communicate back through time. I was going to tell Jesus about it, but he seemed to be more concerned about something else. He had come to save me from something terrible. I had inadvertently been chosen as the body of the beast. The thought 'worship the beast' started beaming from my head. It wasn't me thinking it, though; it was the camera attached to my head.

You can obviously see how confused I had become. But even in my confused state of mind, I knew this wasn't stuff you could go around telling people.

I was scared and felt alone. I had nowhere to hide. This 'thing' followed me wherever I went. I was completely exposed, and it was pure agony. Death has an appeal when you are suffering like this. Luckily I had decided when I was a teenager that suicide is something I could never do. The mess, physical and emotional, that is left behind for other people is simply too destructive. I am sure that God would have forgiven me, but I didn't want to be the cause of anyone else's suffering.

I drew my strength from Scripture. God would never give me a task that was too hard to handle. God wanted me to live, to be wise, to know love, to know the truth. My faith is what saved me from catastrophe.

There are no standard social protocols that tell you how to act in public when you have a mental illness. There's no *Idiot's Guide on How to Be a Schizophrenic*. I had been a fairly normal and reasonably shy kid, but now I had a mental illness, with no instruction manual. Through all my pain, I had nothing to use except my breath and my emotions, and a secret that God revealed to me: 'Just be wrong.' That thought came to me one day from within all the chaos. It's not your usual 'Do this, do that' kind of wisdom, is it? *Who else but God could say something like that?* I thought. I felt that he was telling me, 'Don't pretend you're going to get it right, because you won't.'

Just be wrong. It gave me freedom from the normal human desire to get it right, all of the time, or suffer the consequences.

Within all the chaos, I believed that the world was coming to an end. You can probably understand why I believed that. I thought it was my duty to take that message to the world. And I had this idea that I needed to fulfil a series of things before the end of time could come. To do this I had to correctly interpret every dream I had, and to understand what God really meant in the biblical prophecies. I thought the whole end of time thing depended on me.

With everything else, it was a tremendous weight to carry. My mind was telling me that I had to get every single thought exactly right; otherwise, I could not successfully achieve the mission that God had set before me. I think back on all that mental anguish to get everything right, and I am thankful that now I know the grace of God. 'Just be wrong.'

I have found faith in a way I never had before. When I fell, I fell hard. But God picked me up again and put me right. Even though we don't always know it, God is there working away in our lives.

I'm still a schizophrenic. I take medication for it, and my

various symptoms are mostly under control. The voices of God I hear now are the same voices anyone can hear. They are voices of wisdom, of grace, of acceptance. And of love. I am not perfect, and I don't need to be. I am loved.

Wisdom (Teeth) and the Folly of Anxiety

Nicole Starling

~

Last Friday, I had an appointment to have my wisdom teeth extracted.

As the day approached, I started to get anxious. I promise I *tried* not to think about it too much (although I do admit that I googled the phrase 'wisdom tooth extraction' at one point). But even with the best intentions of pushing the thoughts to the back of my mind, I still felt my heart pound a little harder every time I happened to glance at those same three words in my diary.

By Wednesday night, I started having nightmares. I was in a dentist's chair (it was blood red, not spearmint green), with an overzealous dentist yanking all my teeth out with a gleeful grin on her face. Thursday night was more of the same. Friday morning I woke with a feeling of dread.

Then came the time for my appointment. My husband Dave drove me there, and we sat together in the waiting room. I was really scared. Dave tried to distract me with conversation, but all I could think about was what it would feel like to have a tooth ripped from my mouth.

Then I watched, still feeling sick to the stomach as I saw the patient before me stagger out, clutching the post-tooth extraction instructions in one hand, and what could only have been the extracted tooth in a blue plastic container in the other. His wife's visibly and audibly horrified reaction when she looked in his mouth didn't help my nerves. (A little later, as I was in the chair I heard the dentist talking with her assistant about how close she came to throwing up herself during that particular extraction!)

Then the dentist finally called me in. She took one look in my mouth and decided to change treatment plans. All plans to extract teeth were thrown out, replaced with far less scary-sounding options of fillings and splints. She cleaned my teeth and sent me home.

What a relief! What a let-down! My body didn't know how to cope with all the excess adrenalin surging through it. I also couldn't help but wonder what I was to do with all those cans of soup I had stocked up on the day before.

But it was the *futility* of anxiety that dawned on me as we drove home. This experience reminded me of what a waste of time it can be! There is no point in my worrying about things like wisdom teeth extractions because I do not know what tomorrow will bring—I had spent the last three days making myself into a living illustration of Matthew 6:34!

> *Therefore do not be anxious about tomorrow, for tomorrow will be anxious for itself. Sufficient for the day is its own trouble.* (ESV)

What Kind of Man Is This?

Michael Frost and Alan Hirsch

~

Some time ago, Michael had the opportunity to conduct a regular worship gathering with a group of people who felt uncomfortable in traditional churches. They were an interesting collective of artists, writers and cultural creatives, some of whom had church backgrounds but had rejected it all and others who had never set foot in a church building.

They met for a whole summer in a cramped art gallery above a café. The gallery owners were intrigued by Jesus and had gathered a motley crew of unlikely people together to worship him. Some were unemployed. Some were working only occasionally as artists. Others were suffering with mental illness. Michael and his wife, Carolyn, would lead them through a short, simple liturgy of prayers and music, using uncomplicated symbols like stones, broken pottery, candles, and, of course, bread and wine.

One of the features of the gathering was a brief study of John's Gospel followed by a discussion about the text. John's

Gospel launches right in with John the Baptist's ministry and his identification of Jesus as the Lamb of God, followed quickly by the turning of water into wine at Cana and the cleansing of the temple and Jesus' late-night conversation with Nicodemus about being born again.

What was interesting was how this group approached the text. They immediately saw things that most churched groups don't see. They saw Jesus siding with the oppressed and the marginalised. They read the scenes at the Jordan River as John and Jesus leading the forgotten, the poor and the downtrodden out of the desert through the refreshing waters toward hope and strength. They saw Jesus' transformation of ceremonial waters into wedding wine as his subversive act of taking those religious symbols designed to separate the holy from the unholy and converting them into something delicious for all to enjoy. They identified his fury in the temple as his shattering of the institutional system that denied access and equity to the poor penitents who were forced to change their money and purchase birds for religious sacrifices. They overheard Jesus telling Nicodemus about how the transformation he was initiating began with a transformation of the heart, the inner things over which all people have control, not the outer world, which only the rich or powerful have the capacity to change.

In effect, they read the gospel as being largely about exile and restoration (not that they would have expressed it in these terms). They read it this way because they felt like exiles from institutional religion. To these exiles who felt too dirty to attend church, the Jordan River scenes were a reminder that Jesus is calling everyone, not just the clean, to his side. To these exiles who had been told that they needed to be washed before they could approach God, the wedding at Cana convinced them that in Jesus' kingdom they were welcomed guests and that there was plenty of wine for all. Likewise, to them the cleansing of the temple presented a Jesus who would stop at nothing to demolish every religious hoop put in the way of repentant people accessing God.

In *They Like Jesus but Not the Church,* Dan Kimball reports on similar experiences he has had with unchurched people. The title of the book pretty much sums up his main point and summarises the words of a number of young adults who are drawn to the Jesus of the Gospels who cannot find a place in the church. This has been our experience as well.

Walking on Water

Dorothy O'Neill

~

We sat in a circle reading and discussing the Gospel story of Peter walking on water, 'we' being a women's small group that meets in my house each fortnight.

'That's real faith, faith for miracles,' commented Audrey, a single mum with two teenage children. We all nodded agreement and said that it was a challenge we should take up in our own lives. Two days later Audrey rang me. She sounded very upset.

'My car has broken down and it's going to cost a lot of money to put it right. Money that I just haven't got,' she told me.

I knew her car was an old one and that repairs could only be temporary, but it was a car she needed for work and for her children's needs. We talked about her situation for a few minutes and then I found myself saying, to my astonishment, 'What about "walking on the water" and asking for a new car?'

'A new car! You're joking!' she gasped.

'The stuff of miracles,' I reminded her. 'Let's do it!'

'Well . . . ' she said doubtfully.

Later that day, I found myself thinking of friends in England whom we'd left behind when we migrated as a family to Australia in 1969. Mary had undergone heart surgery. I knew she was recovering but hadn't heard recently how she was doing.

'Why not phone and ask?' came a gentle nudge. Although we had corresponded spasmodically over the years, I had never phoned Mary and Peter from Australia before. The thought persisted, and that night I decided to do so.

The time I had chosen was not good, and I had to wait and wait for a connection. I nearly gave up trying as it was now almost midnight in Australia (though afternoon in England) and I was in bed. However, I felt I must hang in there, and eventually I reached my English friends' home.

Peter answered the phone and I immediately asked after Mary's health. He assured me that she was doing well, and was at that time attending an old scholars' meeting at her local school. That figured—I recalled that Mary usually answered the phone, and I know now that if she had done so on this occasion, the conversation between us would have been very different from the conversation between Peter and me.

What did we talk about? We mainly exchanged news of family and mutual friends, and we also talked about the church in their area which I had once attended. Then, just before we finished speaking, he told me that he had recently sold a piece of land for half-a-million English pounds.

'I'm not sure how to use the money. In fact, it's a burden to me,' Peter told me. Soon after that we finished the call.

It wasn't until the next day that I linked Peter's words about his unexpected windfall with Audrey's need for a car. Could it be that God's answer would come this way? I told Audrey about the phone call and that I now felt increasingly we should follow through in faith. 'Walking on water faith,' I reminded her.

I said that her part was to visit car dealers and decide exactly what car would suit her family's needs. She would then bring me written details and costs, which I would send to my English friends, with a letter placing her needs before them.

Audrey did this, and I wrote to my friends as promised. In my letter I told them that my main desire was that they seek God's direction in the matter. I wrote: 'We are told that God guides us by the peace he gives. Whatever decision you make, let it be the one that brings you peace.'

Two weeks later I received their reply. Here is a quote from the letter: 'We have decided to send you a cheque. We trust that Audrey and many others will benefit from our united act of thought and prayer, as well as from the gift of money. The latter is easy if the heart is in the right place.'

The cheque was generous, and more than covered the cost of a splendid new car which Audrey is still driving—more than ten years later.

Off on the True Track

(From Aussie Pilgrim's Progress)

Kel Richards

‿

Aussie Pilgrim's Progress, *a retelling of John Bunyan's famous classic, narrates a dream about Christian (or Chris for short), from the town of Incendiary, who sets off to find the bush track that leads to God's Own Country. The main impediment to his journey is a disgusting swag on his back. After several adventures that nearly waylay him, he meets a man named Good Will who sets him on the True Track at last.*

Chris was about to set off down the track when he turned back to good ol' Will and said, 'What about this heavy swag on my back? When will I get rid of that? The fact is, I can't get it off my back without help.'

'Don't worry,' Will replied. 'Before long you'll come to the place where burdens are removed, and then it'll be gone in a flash.'

'Good-o,' said Chris, 'if you say so.'

'Now clear off,' said Good Will. 'Show us a clean pair of heels. And keep your eyes open for the Explainer's House. Make sure you call in there on the way past. He's always open to helping passing swaggies, and he has some good stuff you oughta see.'

In my dream I watched as Chris set off down the track. He kept going until he came to a large bungalow by the side of the road. This was the Explainer's House.

Chris is welcomed into the house and the Explainer, a kindly old man, starts to show him around.

The Explainer led Chris into a large front room. The floor and everything in the room was covered with dust. The Explainer called in one of his staff to sweep it clean. The minute this bloke began sweeping the dust flew everywhere, and soon Chris was choking and coughing.

'Sprinkle the room with water,' ordered the Explainer.

The man did this, the dust settled, and then he was able to sweep it away.

'What am I supposed to learn from that little demonstration?' asked Chris, raising one eyebrow.

'It's all symbolic, of course,' said the Explainer. 'This room represents a person's heart. The dust is all the wrongdoing in that person's life. Sweeping without sprinkling the dust first represents the attempt people make to clean up their own lives. But, as you saw, because of the shadow of corruption that lies over the human heart, it achieves nothing—in fact, it ends up worse. The sprinkling represents the difference Jesus makes when he comes into a person's heart. Trusting him deals with the shadow of corruption; his death settles the dust of wrongdoing and cleans it away. Now, here's something that should interest you.'

The Explainer turned on the TV set in the corner and slipped in a DVD. It was an animated cartoon that showed two small boys—brothers. The older was named Passion and the younger was named Patience. Passion was restless but Patience was waiting quietly.

'What's going on here is that their old man has promised them some prezzies,' explained Chris's guide. 'Patience is prepared to wait for his, but Passion can't stand having to wait.' Just then, in the cartoon, the presents were delivered. Passion leaped at his boxes, ripped them open, pulled out the toys and played with them furiously until they were broken.

'All right,' said Chris, 'you'll need to explain this to me.'

'Symbolic again, of course,' said the old man. 'Passion represents the people of this world who want everything now—who live in a world of instant coffee, instant messaging and instant satisfaction. They soon waste what they get. Patience represents Believers—prepared to wait for the good things that are yet to come. When Passion has nothing left but burned up pleasures, Patience will have Paradise.'

'Okay, I get the message,' said Chris. 'Don't get sucked in by all the ads and want everything you see. We're not supposed to live for *this* life and *this* world, but for the life to come and the world to come.'

'You're catching on,' responded the Explainer with a grin. 'Where will you find *true* riches: in the temporary or the permanent (the eternal)? The false promise of materialism is that you find them here and now. That's the falsehood that deceives those who seek wealth, and health, and the good life in this passing world. They want their good things *now*. Bad mistake.'

Then the Explainer showed Chris a model or toy of an old fashioned wood-burning fireplace. In the grate a fire was crackling away merrily. But in front of the fire a tap was constantly squirting water onto it. Despite this the flames didn't go out but blazed as brightly as ever. The Explainer turned the model around to show Chris the secret behind the inextinguishable blaze: behind the wall of the fireplace was a second tap constantly pouring oil onto the fire.

'Interesting,' said Chris again. 'And?'

'Not all that mysterious, really,' said the Explainer. 'The fire represents the heart of the Believer—burning for the truth and burning with commitment to Jesus. The tap spraying water on the fire represents the Evil One (the one our parents and grandparents called Satan or the Devil). The tap pouring oil on the fire to keep it blazing represents Jesus himself. His secret activity in the Believer's heart is what enables the Believer to survive discouragement, persecution, mockery, temptation and whatever else the Dark Forces throw into their attack.'

As they moved on to the next room, the Explainer said, 'And I might add that anyone who thinks this world is not a spiritual battleground between the forces of light and darkness, good and evil, just hasn't been paying attention. Any news bulletin— if you listen with your ears open—will tell you exactly that. Now, here's another thing I want you to see.'

The next DVD was a drama set back in the olden days. On the screen Chris saw a heavily guarded castle. From the happy crowd that could be glimpsed through the windows, it was clear that inside the castle was a good place to be. Outside was another crowd of people who wanted to get in, but there were armed men blocking the doorway and no one was game enough to come near. At last a chap turned up and said, 'Put my name down on the guest list.' A man at a table near the door wrote down the man's name. Then the bloke who'd just arrived put a helmet on his head, drew his sword and charged towards the door. The armed men attacked him and tried to repulse him, but he fought his way through. Once he'd made it past, the door was flung open and he was welcomed in. Inside he was dressed in flowing robes and invited to join the feast at the top table.

'I think I can figure that one out,' said Chris. 'There are forces that will try to keep us from Paradise, but it's worth the most courageous and valiant effort we can make. Is that the lot? Can I get back on the road now?'

'Hang on,' said the Explainer. 'Just one or two more things.'

Next he led Chris into a dark room. In the middle of that room was a miserable looking man locked in an iron cage.

'Who are you?' asked Chris.

'I am what I once was not,' moaned the man.

'Yeah, all right, so who were you once, then?'

'I was once like you: a traveller on the True Track with my heart set on entering God's Own Country.'

'What went wrong?'

'I gave up all attempts at self-control. I chose self-indulgence instead. I turned my back on God. I invited the darkness in.'

'But is there no escape from your iron cage of despair?' asked Chris.

'None!' groaned the man in the cage. 'I eagerly embraced desire, pleasure, profit. I turned my back on Jesus. I ignored him. I said nothing in his defence when my companions mocked him.'

'Well, change again,' urged Chris. 'Turn back.'

'Can't,' whispered the man. 'I don't have the heart. I hardened my heart. Nothing but a lump of stone is left.'

Back at the front door, the Explainer shook Chris's hand and wished him all the best for the journey, adding, 'And may the Comforter go with you, and guide you all the way to God's Own Country.' Chris set out again.

Now in my dream I saw that the track he was on was fenced on both sides. Not many fences have names, but this one did. It was called: God's Rescue.

Chris slogged on, but the heavy swag on his back made the going tough.

At length he came to a small hill. On top of the hill stood a rough, blood-stained wooden Cross; and below was a tomb, cut straight into the rocky hillside.

Chris staggered up the slope, and as he reached the foot of the Cross the straps holding the heavy swag to his back unbuckled themselves. The great weight fell from his shoulders and began to tumble and roll down the hill. It rolled until it fell into the darkness of the rock tomb, and from then on I never saw that heavy burden again. (And neither did Chris!)

The sense of relief that Chris felt was amazing. It wasn't just a weight—it was a shadow that was gone. He said out loud: 'I prayed to you, LORD God, and you healed me, saving me from death and the grave.' For a while he stood there in wonder and amazement, because what had happened just took his breath away.

Chris's prayer is from Psalm 30:2–3.

The Month I Swore Off Devotions

Mandy Smith

'I don't want to die. I just don't want to live for a while.'
Within minutes of hearing this solemn sentence from me, my mum had booked a flight to be with me for a month. So for a while, she helped me live—packing lunches, washing towels. I had taken on too much responsibility for the running of the world and, for a month at least, I was released to just be.

One night during this month, I trudged up the stairs to bed with the sense there was still one more task for my exhausted mind to complete before blessed sleep. It disturbed me to realise the task I dreaded was the process of reading and praying myself into God's presence. So, at that moment, I swore off devotions. I had given the physical work to my mother and I would give the spiritual work to my Father.

In my heart I knew that I read and prayed every night not to make God close, but to make myself aware of his closeness. But it took a lot of work, putting off the cares of the day, focusing on the truths of Scripture, journalling, praying without wandering or snoozing. Wouldn't it be easier to just stop and be aware of his closeness? So for a month I brushed my teeth, turned out the light and just basked for a bit. I didn't say anything or ask him to say anything. I just trusted that he was there, that he was good, that he loved me and that that was enough. The darkness all around me was God. The silence was God. The sleep was God.

After my month I resurrected some of the more structured spiritual disciplines. But they were different now. I did them for a new reason and with more creativity because I had had a month-long holiday with my Father. And, as my mum and I reminisce about a month of life together, even still my Father and I draw from those shared experiences. And I'm okay with living again.

Lost in Translation

Paul O'Rourke

Roger Ellem is known around Australia as 'Mr Compassion'. Thanks to his passionate advocacy over three decades, around 12,000 children in the developing world have been sponsored by Australians through the development agency Compassion Australia. In this work he has travelled to some sixty countries, which has left him with a veritable encyclopaedia of traveller's tales.

You need a sense of humour when you travel, especially in the developing world. Roger recalls one occasion when he went to a resort in Africa's Rift Valley for an afternoon to break a long journey.

'Some American guests left the door of a room open and were delighted when three monkeys came in—until they took a lady's bags and scampered off into the nearest tree. The lady's underwear cascaded slowly down from the branches and into the river.'

You just can't take things seriously all the time, says Roger—especially where language is concerned.

'The first lesson I learned in this regard was when Margaret and I were missionaries in Bangladesh. Our senior missionary, who had been there more than twenty-six years, thought he spoke the local language like a native. He didn't.

'His favourite sermon was "Christ, the light of the world", which he preached whenever he had an opportunity. The only problem was that the word for light, *alo*, is very similar to the word for potato, *alu*. Our senior missionary got the two mixed up, so astonished congregations heard him proclaim Christ "the potato of the world", and speak about the need for Christians to let their potatoes shine.

'He would say, "The church needs shining potatoes. Is your potato shining?" The congregation would shake their heads, and this would start him off again. Because he was the senior missionary, they either said nothing or agreed with him.

'I once asked him, "Did you mean to say what you said?" He replied, "Are you trying to correct my Bengali?" I said, "I think you've said something wrong." He replied, "When you've been in this country as long as I have, then you can correct my Bengali. Until then, keep quiet."

'So there we were, defending the cause of shining potatoes.'

Another of Roger's colleagues once recounted the story of the feeding of the five thousand from Matthew 14. But instead of telling the audience that Jesus got five thousand people to sit on the grass, he told them Jesus made fifty people, in groups of one hundred, climb up a tree.

'It's easy to make mistakes. A senior Compassion worker in Indonesia was asked to speak at a function following a welcome by the local head man. The head man spoke at length, and very well.

'Our Compassion man stood up to thank the *kapala* ("head man"). Unfortunately, he used the word *kalapa* instead, which means "coconut". He told the group that they should listen to this coconut and be thankful for this coconut, for there were very few coconuts as wise as this one and Indonesia needed more wise coconuts.

'By then the head man had a fit of the giggles. He could have been very offended, but he recognised the guest's heart was good.'

Sometimes language problems can be even more embarrassing, as Roger discovered when he was in Brazil with an Australian sponsor.

'She came from a Plymouth Brethren background and by any definition was prim and proper. One day she decided she wanted an ornamental decoration for her house, a kind of stylised piranha fish she'd seen somewhere. Being the person she was, she insisted on going shopping on her own.

'She started at the bottom of a row of shops, learning her Portuguese from a dictionary. She kept asking for what she thought was a "dried fish". The first shopkeeper was indignant and virtually threw her out of his shop. She went into about six shops repeating the same thing.

'Finally, a shopkeeper took her at her word and asked her to wait. Some time later, a disreputable, toothless man came out. "Here's the prostitute you've been asking for," the shopkeeper said.

'Instead of using the correct term for the fish souvenir, *piranha empalhada* ("fish stuffed with straw"), she had used the normal Portuguese word for "dry" and asked for *piranha seca*— not realising this was actually slang for "slim prostitute".'

Someone usually ends up paying for language faux pas like these—in this case literally. The man had taken a shower, shaved and changed his clothes, and he wasn't going anywhere until the woman paid him for his time.

Language isn't the only cause of embarrassment. Culture shock also does strange things to people. On one trip Roger led to Africa, a street shoeshine boy polished an Australian pastor's shoe. 'At the end of the conversation, the pastor wasn't sure what to do, so he opened his wallet and allowed the boy to take a note. It just happened to be a $US100 bill. It must have been the most expensive shoe shine in history.'

Food too presents frequent interesting challenges. Roger makes a rule of never asking what he is eating because sometimes it is better not to know.

'It was our final night in a northern Thailand Akha village. We had a special meal which was very nice. One team member demanded to know what the meat was, only to discover we had just eaten the two dogs we had spent the last three days playing with.'

Sometimes, though, it's not possible to avoid knowing what you're being served, as Roger found on a trip to Kazakhstan with pastors connected with the Australian Baptist Missionary Society.

'We were invited to an indigenous homestead for a meal. Khazaks traditionally live in a *yurt*, something like an Indian tepee but significantly bigger. We sat together on the floor, and, being the oldest of the group, I was placed at the head of the table.

'We had seen them spit-roasting a sheep when we came in and the appetising smell wafted through the tent. We were all looking forward to a lovely mutton meal. But when the time came, everyone was served except the husband of the household and me. We were to be fed last as a sign of honour.

'Finally, with a flourish and a great deal of ceremony, they put down in front of me the boiled head of the sheep with the eyes still intact. I was expected to scoop out the eyes and eat them. I can tell you that boiled sheep's head is a wretched-looking thing.

'So while the rest of the team tucked into spit-roasted sheep, I had to stop myself from gagging as I enthusiastically scooped out the eyes and downed them. It would have been a huge insult to have refused.'

Julian's Story

Sheridan Voysey

~

I have seen the power and values of heaven touch and change our world. Whether it's a former brothel madam encountering God and deciding to run a refuge for girls coming off the street, or an entrepreneur training poor business owners to grow their ventures and employ others, followers of Christ are working to make this world more like the world to come. And God is often performing miracles in the process.

I remember meeting Julian for the first time at a church in Perth, Western Australia. I was speaking from the platform and Julian was sitting in one of the front rows. He had recently encountered God, had been brought to church by a friend, and because he wasn't yet familiar with typical church 'protocol', continued interrupting me with his questions. Julian had some great thoughts and I'm glad he ignored his friend's encouragement to sit quietly like everyone else.

Over the next few months I really enjoyed talking with Julian and exploring some of his questions about God and

Christian life. Sometimes I'd see him crying in church, simply thankful for what Christ was doing in his life.

Julian was an attractive man with styled black hair and a ballroom dancer's build. Yet his face was often pale, a little sunken, and at times he looked too thin. And we discovered the reason. Julian was HIV-positive—he had AIDS. During an operation to remove a collapsed lung, Julian had acquired the virus from a transfusion of contaminated blood. His white blood cells were now being destroyed, making his immune system weak and leaving Julian open to sickness and ultimately death.

Julian rang me one day. 'I've come across this bit in the Bible,' he said. 'Can I read it to you?' He flicked open to the page and read from the book of James:

> *Is any one of you sick? He should call the elders of the church to pray over him and anoint him with oil in the name of the Lord. And the prayer offered in faith will make the sick person well; the Lord will raise him up. If he has sinned, he will be forgiven. Therefore confess your sins to each other and pray for each other so that you may be healed. (James 5:14–16)*

'So,' he said, returning to me, 'what do you think about that?'

'I think we need to make some phone calls!' I replied. I called around the leaders of the church and arranged a time for us to pray for Julian's healing.

Later that week we gathered in a small room in the church complex. We had the oil ready—a symbol of God's Spirit who heals. We had the leaders ready—as we were directed to. We sat Julian in a seat and, along with some of his close friends, gathered around and placed our hands on his shoulders. In the privacy of this confidential group, Julian confessed to God the sins of his past. Then each of us took turns in asking God to heal our friend. Finally, oil was placed on Julian's forehead and the senior pastor of the church said, 'Julian, be healed in the name of Jesus.' There was a great sense of anticipation in the room. It felt like a divine moment.

Well, it's always a risk praying like that. You're never quite sure what God will do as, ultimately, miracles are up to him. But it was with some expectation that Julian went for his next round of monthly blood tests.

The results came back. Julian's white blood cells had decreased even further. He was getting worse, not better.

The following month's tests also gave little encouragement. This time the white blood cells hadn't dropped any further, but they hadn't increased either. There was more prayer in church and at home with friends. But we wondered whether God had already given us his answer.

Then Julian went for his next round of tests, the third after that original prayer meeting. The doctor looked incredulously at the printed report and said some sort of mistake must have happened during the procedure. He arranged for another blood test to double-check. But those results came back the same. The virus was no longer evident in Julian's body. His white blood cell count was normal. There was now no trace of HIV whatsoever in Julian's system.

Julian had been healed of AIDS.

I lost touch with Julian for a while and then, about a year later, a hand touched my shoulder as I sat in a coffee shop. I turned around and hardly recognised the person behind me. It was Julian, but where his face had once looked sunken and pale, his complexion and features were now full, healthy and tanned. The healing had stayed. And the doctors were still amazed.

Heaven is not yet with us, that's for certain. But in the meantime God is changing this world to make it more like the new world that's coming. Through miracles like Julian's, we glimpse that future place where scars of mind are healed and wounds of body are made right. And as I discovered anew through Julian's experience, God calls his followers to be part of the action.

Chapter Two of My Life

Philip Yancey

~

I had spent a lovely weekend in Los Alamos, New Mexico, speaking to a unique church that combines six different denominations. My wife Janet had travelled with me so much during a book tour the previous few months that she felt obligated to stay home and do her duties at the senior centre where she works, so I went alone. My New Mexico hosts met me in Taos for a delightful day of bam-bam bump skiing on Thursday, then we drove together to Los Alamos.

It's quite a place, created in the 1940s for the Manhattan Project, and the fabled home of the atomic bomb. The town has more PhDs per capita than any place in the world. I had a fascinating meeting with some of the physicists and other scientists from the lab during which we discussed matters of science and faith and nuclear terrorism and pacifism and other weighty issues. Friday night I spoke on my book *Prayer: Does It Make Any Difference?*—a very appropriate topic in view of what follows. Saturday I did a seminar consisting of three one-hour lectures and a book signing, and then took off early Sunday morning for Denver, where I planned to meet Janet for a friend's wedding.

I was driving alone on a remote highway, curvy but not too hilly, at about 100 kilometres an hour. A curve came up suddenly and I turned to the left, perhaps too sharply. Ford Explorers are rather notorious for fishtailing, and this one did. I tried to correct, but as best as I can reconstruct what happened, my tyre slipped off the edge of the asphalt onto the dirt. That started the Explorer rolling over sideways, at least three times and probably more. Amazingly, the vehicle stopped right side up. All windows were blown out, and skis, boots, laptop computer and suitcases were strewn over 30 metres or so in the dirt. I tried my hands and legs and they worked fine. I was able to unbuckle the seat belt and walk away. Within five minutes a couple of cars stopped and their occupants, Mormons on the way to church, called for help.

I had a lot of minor cuts and bruises on my face and limbs, but except for a persistent nosebleed, nothing serious. I did have intense pain in my neck, though. When the ambulance came, they strapped me into a rigid body board, taping my head still and immobilising it with a neck brace. It took almost an hour to reach the town of Alamosa in southern Colorado.

Looking back now, I see so many mini-miracles that all contributed to a good outcome. The Mormons (two of whom were trained in emergency medicine) travelling that route on a Sunday morning. The most experienced X-ray/MRI technician, normally off on weekends, filling in for a sick colleague. The ER doctor, featured that day on the cover of the local paper, a graduate of the University of Michigan medical school, who had just returned to his small town in Colorado to be of service. And, most of all, the injury itself.

Alamosa has no radiologist on duty over the weekend, so all images had to be modemed to Australia (where it was Monday morning) for interpretation. The images are so dense that the high-speed transmittal takes an hour, and then the diagnosis can take another hour. After the initial batch, the doctor came in with those prefatory words no patient wants to hear: 'There's no easy way to say this, Mr. Yancey . . . ' I had broken the C-3 vertebra in a 'comminuted' fashion. (I didn't know that word either; look it up and the dictionary says 'pulverised'.) The good news was that the break did not occur in the spinal cord column itself. If it had, well, C-2 is where Christopher Reeve's break occurred, so you get the picture of what can happen up there. The spinal column has three channels, one for the spinal cord, and two for arterial blood supply, which is where my fracture occurred. The bad news was that due to the splintered nature of the break, a bone fragment may well have nicked or penetrated an artery.

'We have a jet standing by if needed to airlift you to Denver,' the doctor explained. 'We'll do another MRI, this time with an iodine dye solution to reveal any possible leakage from the artery. This is a life-threatening situation.'

Meanwhile Janet, whom I had called from the ambulance, had scrambled to throw things together and begin the drive to Alamosa (four hours from our home in Denver) to be with me. Our Good Samaritan neighbour Mark insisted on going with her, a magnificent gift as it freed her to make phone calls and compose herself during that tense drive. They were about halfway to Alamosa when the doctor gave her this news via phone, explaining that if they found arterial leakage they could not hold the plane for her; I would be shipped immediately. You would have to use a cell phone in Colorado to understand some of the tension here: about every third word gets dropped and, in the mountains, the call cuts off every thirty seconds or so. Poor Janet was trying to decide whether to turn around and drive back to Denver or continue on to Alamosa, with the possibility of watching my jet contrails in the sky above her.

I went in for the iodine-dye scan, and then was left alone to wait for the transmission to Australia and the results. In all, I lay strapped onto that body board for seven hours. The emergency room was quite busy that day, mostly crying babies. I had plenty of time to think. I've done articles on people whose lives have been changed overnight by an accident that left them paraplegic or quadriplegic. Evidently I had narrowly missed that fate; and I mean narrowly—my break was about one-half inch from the spinal cord. However, if my artery was leaking, an artery that feeds the brain, or if it threw a clot, well, a fate worse than paralysis awaited me.

I stayed calm throughout, my pulse holding steady around seventy. And as I lay there, contemplating what I had just been teaching in Los Alamos about prayer, and facing the imminent possibility of death for the first time, I felt very peaceful. I reflected on what a wonderful life I have had, with a life-giving marriage partner of thirty-seven years, all but three of Colorado's fifty-four 14,000-foot mountains under my belt, adventures in more than fifty countries, work that allows me both meaning and total freedom. Just that weekend I had heard again story after story of people who have been touched by one of my books. I looked back on my life and felt no regrets (well, I would like to get those last three '14ers' climbed). And as I thought of what may await me, I felt a feeling of great trust. No one raised in the kind of church environment I grew up in totally leaves behind the acrid smell of fire and brimstone, but I felt an overwhelming sense of trust in God. I have come to know a God of compassion and mercy and love. I have no clue what heaven or an afterlife will be like but I felt sustained by that trust. OK, the morphine drip was beginning to kick in too!

Those were the tense hours: Janet riding down the road with our neighbour, feeling helpless and unsure, with scenes of how her life would change with a dead or paralysed husband; and me utterly helpless, strapped on a table with the images that would determine my future bouncing off some satellite en route to Australia.

As it happened, thank God—oh, yes, thank God—the results were far better than either of us could imagine. The MRI revealed no arterial leakage. I was released within half an hour of Janet's arrival, fitted with a rigid neck brace that would keep my head from moving for the next ten weeks or so.

We got a hot meal, my first of the day, and began the drive back home. Before midnight I was sitting in a bathtub discovering new cuts and abrasions, warming up and getting ready for a challenging night's sleep in my own bed.

I remember sitting in the seat of the Ford Explorer as it finally stopped rolling, with its engine still running, and thinking, *This begins chapter two of my life.* Indeed it did, though with considerably brighter prospects than it seemed at the time. I hope to ski long mogul runs again, and I have another chance to climb those last three '14ers', to gaze at the wild flowers along the way, to cherish friends and love my wife and family and thank God for every minute of this precious gift of life.

Philip Yancey's accident occurred in February 2007, and this article was written shortly afterwards. By 15 August that year he had finally climbed the last of Colorado's '14ers'.

The Ever-Shrinking Keynote

Nola Passmore

~

A couple of years ago, I applied to present a keynote address at a conference in Boston. The submission guidelines indicated that the presentation should be an hour in length, so I prepared my application with that in mind. My proposal was accepted, but due to the large number of submissions, the speaking time was reduced to thirty minutes. I knew it would be a challenge to say everything I wanted to say in that time, but I agreed. I could certainly understand that they had a lot of papers to accommodate in their program.

However, when the schedule came out, I found that I had only been allocated fifteen minutes.

I checked the other presentations and discovered that I was the only person in the whole program who had been given such a short time. Everyone else had at least half an hour. Confident that this must surely be a mistake, I emailed the conference organising team and politely queried the time I had been given. To my dismay, I was informed that it wasn't a mistake. They had received more submissions than they had expected and unfortunately the time allocated to some papers had to be reduced.

I could understand that, but why was I the only person who had been allocated fifteen minutes?

By this time, I was feeling pretty disappointed and angry. I was giving up my time at a very busy part of the year, I was travelling to the other side of the world, and I was paying the bulk of the expenses myself—all for a fifteen-minute presentation.

I contemplated writing back and complaining about the situation, but as I prayed, I felt the Lord remind me of two passages in Scripture. The first was Matthew 19:30: 'But many who are now first will be last, and many who are now last will be first' (GNB). The second was the parable of the wedding feast in Luke 14:7–11. Jesus was at the home of one of the Pharisees and he noticed how they were all jostling for the best seats. He told them that when they were invited to a wedding feast, they should not take the place of honour because a more important person may have been invited and they may have to give up their seat. Instead, they should take the lowest place, so that the host could move them to a better position and they could be honoured in front of everyone.

After meditating on these Scriptures, I felt that God wanted me to humbly accept the time that had been given to me.

Even then, I couldn't help thinking that it was still a mistake.

So when I emailed the conference organisers again, I thanked them for clarifying the situation and said that I would prepare a fifteen-minute talk. I thought that once they saw the fifteen minutes mentioned again, they would realise their error. But no—there was no reply saying that a mistake had been made.

I reconciled myself to the fact that I had only been given a very short time. Knowing that I couldn't possibly say everything I needed to, I decided to write a longer paper to hand out at the conference. At least they would be able to read the full text, even if I could only note a few highlights in my talk.

Two days before I was due to catch my flight to Boston, the organisers sent a new copy of the schedule to all of the presenters. To my amazement, my time had been increased to forty-five minutes! I now had a longer speaking time than many other presenters. The talk went well and I was able to hand out my paper to about one hundred people. I would never have written the entire paper if I knew I was going to have the extra time, so that turned out to be a blessing too.

At the end of the conference, I ran into the only other Australian delegate. While we were having a chat, the conference organiser came over and joined us. She said that she had asked her staff who their favourite presenters were and they had told her the two Australians. However, it wasn't our presentation skills or the content of our papers that had impressed them. We were their favourites because of the way we had treated them and because nothing they had asked of us was seen as too much trouble. Apparently, some of the other presenters had treated them like the 'hired help'.

This was quite humbling for me. I certainly hadn't felt very gracious when I'd been told I only had fifteen minutes.

This story reminds me again of the importance of trying to respond to every situation as Jesus would. He gave up everything he was entitled to in heaven and humbled himself, coming to earth as a servant so that we could be saved through his death on the cross. Following his example sometimes means that we will have a lower place in the eyes of the world, but Jesus holds us in high esteem. His love and acceptance are all that matters.

Seven Days, Seven Dollars

Az Hamilton

⁓

The idea came about after a conversation I had with a friend about the statistics on poverty—those ridiculous figures that seemed impossible to comprehend. What does it mean for 600 million children to live off $1 or less a day? And the global food crisis brings up more hard-to-grasp numbers. One hundred million people forced into extreme poverty because the cost of living is going up. How do you get your head around that?

I'm youth communicator for Compassion Australia and I love being able to rattle off the stats. But unless we can communicate the reality of what's really going on, it's just words.

My idea was *7 Days 7 Dollars*. Could I live for a whole week off a dollar a day, like 12 per cent of the world does? The goal was to step inside their lives for a week, to see how it feels—and in the process to raise awareness about the desperate need.

People in a lot of the developing world are now paying the

same price for food as we are—except we earn hundreds or even thousands and they earn maybe a dollar a day. So if they live like this every day, was it possible for me to live like that here in Australia?

With $7 I made my way to the supermarket on Day 1. Half way there it dawned on me I didn't have spare money for petrol, so I pulled over and walked the rest of the way. At the supermarket I bought my week's supply of food: rice, two-minute noodles, pasta, milk and four soy sauce sachets. I soon discovered that poverty is really a lack of choice. The same food every day. The same routine every day.

As the week went on, I eliminated other luxuries from my house. On Day 3 I stopped using tap water. I walked to a local park, collected bore water and boiled it so I could drink it. Even then I was challenged. Unclean water is the number one killer in the world—1.8 million die annually from diarrhoea alone. My twenty-minute walks every day were still easier than drinking disease-infested water.

On Day 5 I eliminated technology, media, TV, music, reading—anything that entertained. Even the internet, which was tough for a Facebook addict. I abandoned the luxury of a toilet and dug a hole in the backyard. Did you know that half a billion children don't have access to toilets?

The week was an incredible eye opener. It showed me how much we spend on junk. We consume without thought over and over again. The whole time I was thinking about that final day—thinking, *It'll be OK because Saturday is coming and I'll be able to eat normally again. I'll have food with flavour!*

This simple thought process challenged me beyond anything else throughout the week. I was returning to normality, but other people are living like this forever. I lost five kilograms in one week. If I lived like that for a year, I'd be skin and bone.

By the end of the week, I was done. I was finished. I was cranky. I was over it.

But reality sank in. I was in Australia. I had so much. What does that mean for me? Do I have a responsibility to do something?

7 Days 7 Dollars. It can be done, but it's not easy. It's only when you truly feel what it's like to be without choice that you realise how easy it is to make a difference.

A full video diary of Az's 7 Days 7 Dollars week can be seen at his website, <http://www.500dreads.com>.

Saved Letters

Irene Voysey

❧

A few years after I became a Christian, I was sent to my birthplace, Bangalore, on an assignment. My family and I had left India when Bangalore was still called the Garden City of India, long before it was invaded by call centres and Industry—yes, with a capital I. Today, according to Wikipedia, Bangalore is called the *Silicon Valley of India* and is the fastest growing major metropolis in the country.

I took a day off during my assignment there, hired a rattling taxi and set out to visit the place where I spent the first seventeen years of my life: a gold mining area called Kolar Gold Fields, once famous for having the deepest mine in the world.

Our old house was still there, now occupied by two families, and I followed the familiar road past it. When we kids were home from boarding school in Bangalore, our family walked this road on Sundays as we went to and from church. St Michael and All Angels was still there, looking rather forlorn, but still proudly bearing its dramatic name.

Memories flooded back of a blue banner with a handsome St Michael, his foot triumphantly placed on the dragon's head, and of my father reading in a firm, confident voice from a big Bible supported by a rather terrifying brass eagle. At least it had seemed terrifying to a little girl in the congregation. I remembered Dad going off regularly to something called Parish Council. I guess his skills as an accountant must have been put to good use there, but to me it was all very mysterious.

As I stood in the dusty grounds, now devoid of flowering shrubs, I wondered whether my father, who died at forty-eight, really understood and believed in what he used to read aloud from the Bible. We never discussed spiritual things at home, although we always said grace before meals: 'For what we are about to receive, may the Lord make us truly thankful. Amen.' True, that was an era when religion, sex and politics were not discussed in polite society. It was taken for granted that babies would be christened, and in due course would be Confirmed in their faith, with us girls wearing new white dresses and loving every minute in our mysterious white veils. I remember feeling very holy on the day of my Confirmation, yet it wasn't until forty years later that I came to truly understand and embrace the faith my lips had professed at St Michael's so long ago.

With all my heart I longed to know if my Dad had embraced it too. We had a strong bond, and my children were surprised to find that I had saved the letters he wrote to me at some important times of my life: the week before my high school exams in Bangalore; then later, the time we lived in a boarding house in North Sydney while Dad finished working out his contract in India; and another letter encouraging me to enjoy life when I ventured out of Australia on my own, to Lae, PNG. The last letter was sent to me in Darwin, written with a great deal of forgiving love and grace, even though he'd sat for three hours by our neighbour's phone (we didn't have one), waiting for the call I'd promised to make but had forgotten about because I was partying. Then Dad was gone and there were no more loving letters.

I often wondered whether we would meet again before the throne of God, even though I believe that we will each have to answer to God if we choose to treat him as an optional extra in our lives. Was God just a legend in an ancient book for my Dad? Or perhaps a god with Alzheimer's, the memory of our wrong words and deeds wiped out of his mind—benevolently ready to reward us all with the joys of heaven; his famous role as a righteous and supreme Judge a farce; his Son who paid the penalty for our sins as lifeless as the cross on the church building? I hoped my father had not trusted in such illogical nonsense.

Last year, a few weeks after my mother went to heaven, I went to Perth. I needed a few laughs and my childhood friend in Perth never fails to provide those. I also spent a couple of days with an older cousin, a retired clergyman, whom I hadn't seen for decades. Over our first cuppa he asked, 'Have I ever shown you the letter your Dad wrote to me when I informed all the family that I was going into the ministry?' I hadn't seen it, so he got up and fetched the fifty-nine year old letter. I grinned as I opened the short typewritten sheets (no A4 back then!) and saw the familiar type-face of Dad's portable Olivetti.

Then, as I began reading the letter, my grin faded and tears began to flow down my face. My father had written: 'How does it come about that you made such a choice? Personally, I don't think you made it at all . . . I don't think things have changed much, even in this Jet Age, from the time the Master walked the shores of Galilee and chose His little band. I am of the opinion that He still chooses those He wants to teach and preach His Holy Gospel, so you see my boy, when He called, you had but to obey . . .'

So my Dad *had* understood the Bible, and he too had believed in Jesus! My happy tears eventually stopped and my cousin and I laughed together, amazed at how our loving God had answered this prayer deep in my heart.

I was leaving the next day, so my cousin agreed that I should borrow the letter and photocopy it. A week later, when he phoned for a chat, I told him that my father's original letter was in an envelope by the front door, ready to be posted back to him in the morning.

Before I left to post the letter the next day, there was a phone call from my cousin's daughter in Perth. She said, 'Irene, I'm sorry to have to tell you that Dad died suddenly last night.'

And so I still have that original letter, signed by my father, now a priceless legacy from both him and my cousin—who, I am confident, will be laughing with me and our parents one day before the throne of our infinitely loving God.

A Man Who Embodied Jesus

Michael Frost and Alan Hirsch

~

*A*lan Walker was an Australian evangelist and theologian born in 1911 who devoted his life to both social activism and evangelism.

In the 1950s Walker launched a three-year-long evangelistic tour across Australia and New Zealand in which he preached to more than half the total populations of each country. Evangelistic rallies like this were relatively common in Australia at the time; by the early twentieth century, fundamentalist preachers from the United States had begun regular visits to the country to conduct similar evangelism circuits. But the scale of Walker's itinerary was unique in that he heralded the integration of evangelism and social activism in a day when the Protestant church generally saw the two realms as incompatible.

He also had the moral courage to be an outspoken critic of the racist 'White Australia' policy as early as 1938, when the church had been largely silent on the issue. As a pacifist during World War II, and the Vietnam War, he attracted the ire of the media but remained true to his convictions. After his last evangelical tour in 1958, he took over the leadership of the Methodist Central Mission in Sydney and developed it into one of the country's largest social justice agencies.

He was expelled twice from South Africa for his anti-apartheid stance and was knighted by the Queen of England, befriended by Martin Luther King Jr, and dubbed 'the conscience of the nation' by the Governor-General of Australia. Alan Walker embodied Jesus because his social activism was never at the expense of his evangelistic passion; 'Let it never be forgotten that it is Christ we offer.'

Not Snail Mail, Not Email but . . .

Anusha Atukorala

~

Several times a day, I come to my computer with glad anticipation. Any guesses as to what draws me to it? My eagerness knows no bounds; what I anticipate fills me with a warm glow inside. It's the thought of getting fresh new emails.

When I reach my computer and eagerly click onto Outlook each day, many fresh messages bounce into my inbox. Oh, what a thrill they give me! The emails from family and friends always bring a smile to my face and joy to my heart.

How exciting it is to connect with someone far away. It might be ten kilometres or three thousand, the distance does not matter a whit and is fast covered. Receipt is instant. A reply can be instantaneous too, no matter how great the distance. A deep link is forged. I feel 'rich' in being connected to others.

I was reflecting the other day that God sends me mail all the time. I don't have to go two or three times a day to a machine to receive it. The amazing fact is that if I am open to his voice and his ways, I receive it all the day long.

Sometimes I get mail from him through his marvellous creation. It may be in a beautiful sunrise or a breathtaking sunset. It could be in the sound of the birds sweetly chirping in the trees. On occasion, it's been through a rainbow that startlingly fills my vision, giving me fresh, beautiful evidence of God's love and care for me.

Many times it comes in the quiet pleasure I receive as I walk along the green scenic paths in my neighbourhood, drinking in the loveliness around me. God's mail also reaches me when I walk on the seashore and gaze at the huge expanse of the ocean, catching a glimpse of the amazing vastness of my God. What does he whisper through the wonderful and beautiful world he has created ? He tells me he loves me; he tells me he is my Creator; he tells me he is in control. And he tells me he is the author of everything good.

There are times when God's mail comes through a sibling, my mum or a friend—when they phone or write to me or send me an unexpected card or greeting. Their love, friendship and concern for me remind me of the richness God has brought into my life through others. A phone call when I am down, at the right time, makes me aware that God reaches me often through others. They—we—are his hands and feet.

Sometimes, God's mail even comes through adversity. Adversity makes me seek God more and so it often turns into an unexpected blessing. My need becomes a way that God can reach me, teach me and bring me closer to himself.

114

And so it is something vital, even necessary, for my own spiritual growth.

Sometimes God speaks to me when I turn the pages of his Word. His gracious and loving promises strike me and wash over me and fill me with hope. That's really precious mail from him. It nourishes my soul.

Then there are different circumstances—good or bad, happy or sad—that make me realise he is working in my life. Circumstances are another kind of mail from God.

There are so many different ways that my Creator and Saviour speaks to me in a day, and it fills me with wonder and joy. I've got *God-mail* today and my cup runs over.

I Don't Know

John Mallison

At the conclusion of our studies in theological college, the Principal gathered us exit students together in his lounge room and gave us a farewell message. In it he included three words that have remained with me ever since. He said, 'We have sought to help you develop a sound knowledge and understanding of a broad spectrum of subjects which will equip you in fulfilling your call as pastors. However you will encounter many puzzling questions in your own mind, or raised by those you seek to help cope with the mysteries and traumas of life, which you will feel ill-equipped to answer adequately. Be honest with people when you don't understand. Don't hesitate to say, "*I don't know!*" '

In my pastoring of people in diverse situations I have freely used those words time and again.

So much happens in this world for which I don't have an answer. I have ministered to so many godly people, often close friends, who have blessed a multitude by their Christ-like love expressed so freely and sacrificially but whose own lives have now been devastated by a stroke, dementia, an aggressive cancer unresponsive to treatment, a traffic accident or other such crushing situations. They may or may not have asked 'why?' but in seeking to uphold and encourage them I make it clear that I struggle to make sense of innocent suffering—that as to why it happens, 'I don't know'. During my prayers with them I frankly admit to God my confusion at what has taken place.

I find myself also using those three words with those I come alongside who are struggling with rejection and isolation, which are often the way life feels for a huge number of people. And there are so many more kinds of suffering that I don't understand—such as the injustice experienced by the poor and needy or suffering caused by natural disasters, wars, conflicts and economic downturns.

In those three words, 'I don't know', our Principal was not encouraging us to be uncertain about our faith but to be open and honest about what we didn't understand, especially about life's troubles and pain. In every situation, despite our inability to fully comprehend all life's complex experiences, there is always hope, especially for those who seek to take Jesus Christ and his teachings seriously.

Yes, I still *don't know* how to explain much of what we experience in this world. Likewise, there is still much *I don't know* about the God of this world, the Sovereign Lord of the universe. However, of this I am convinced about his character:

God is boundless love, undeservedly kind, totally good, all-powerful, ever present, all-knowing, benevolent, genuine, fully aware of and well able and desirous to meet all our needs.

After confessing to others what '*I don't know*', I can then, based on this big idea of God, confidently but lovingly and gently share words of hope. For the true Christ-follower there is always hope.

'Mr Eternity'

Brad Baker

~

Let me take you back to 1939. It was a freezing cold and windy July morning, and chiming like the bells of doom, the eerie echoes of the Sydney Town Hall clock had just confirmed it was 5.00 am. Among the cold and bleak man-made canyons of steel and glass, a shadowy figure in a grey felt hat and dark blue suit was ambling along, driven by an insatiable desire.

As he moved with practised stealth from shadow to shadow, he reflected on his pitiful childhood.

Born in Balmain in 1884, with both parents drunkards, he had two brothers and two sisters who lived much of their time either in jail or overseeing the sisters' brothels they had illegally established in the narrow alleyways of a bustling young city. Living from scraps of food found in garbage cans, stealing milk from unsuspecting doorsteps and being jailed himself for living in a fog of alcohol at the tender age of fifteen were vivid

119

reminders of a past that haunted him and fuelled his need for retribution.

Miraculously he had survived to adulthood and was now fifty-seven years of age. The same city that had been his only schoolyard had barely emerged from the depths of the Great Depression and was about to enter into a war in Europe that would soon claim the lives of millions.

He was of a slight build and only just over five feet tall, but as he trod the empty, barren footpaths he was undaunted by the potential threats to life and limb that could emerge from every alley or darkened doorway he silently drifted past. The urge to achieve his mission far outweighed the possibly gruesome fate that could befall him at every turn.

Finally he arrived, stopped and glanced around furtively to ensure he was alone. Then he bent to the ground, reached into his pocket and removed a sharpened object. With a much practised and fluid motion, he struck out at the concrete, and in an instant his mission was accomplished. Rising in triumph, he hastily retreated into the shadows from which he had come, anxious that his anonymity be preserved.

Some hours later, as the city emerged from its slumber and its citizens, as yet unaware of what drama the day would bring, began to attend to their daily duties, a constable was stopped by a young lady at the entrance to a train station. She pointed to the concrete and said, 'Look, there it is again!' The constable moved in for a closer inspection and saw a single word, written with chalk in perfect copperplate script: *Eternity*. It was a word that would become synonymous with this city, continuing to reappear mysteriously for the next thirty years, created by the slight man in the grey felt hat.

Arthur Stace was this one-word missionary, and his story is far more intriguing and complex than the brief glimpse I have given above. It all began when Arthur was enticed, with the thought of a free cup of tea and a rock cake, to attend a Baptist church hall meeting in Darlinghurst in 1937. There he listened to the evangelist John Ridley, a Military Cross winner in the First World War.

Ridley inspired Arthur with his passion for the lost when he cried out, 'Where will you spend eternity? I wish I could shout "ETERNITY!" through all the streets of Sydney!' Arthur knew, then and there, that he had been given a mission by God. Until he died at the age of eighty-four, Arthur continued to faithfully carry out and live for this mission.

This single-minded, one-word missionary was immortalised sixty years later in glowing letters made of steel and neon, letters that were many times greater than his own height, splashed across the very bridge that symbolised this great city in the year it hosted the Olympic Games. The word then seen by almost two billion people was simply: *Eternity*.

We will never know how many people who read Arthur's elegant, flowing script, or who subsequently heard the details of his dramatic life, actually stopped to consider his message, and to what extent it changed their lives. But the story of Arthur Stace, 'Mr Eternity', is certainly a unique part of Australia's Christian heritage that is worth preserving.

Life on the Flip Side

Mandy Smith

~

Australians are often reminded that we live on the flip side. We know that much of the world's population calls our country 'Down Under'. And we regularly have to adjust for the fact that the rest of the developed world up there in the northern hemisphere is doing things very differently.

We're aware that we're upside-down as we sing European carols about snow while we're sweating in an Australian Christmas. And we realise that we're upside-down when we watch American TV shows about pumpkins and autumn leaves while spring is in full swing. I didn't even understand the connection between Easter and the rebirth of spring until I moved to the northern hemisphere. When I was a kid in Australia, Easter was in the autumn and everything was dying.

But now, from my spot here 'up over', as I reflect on the seasons of life, I'm aware that I'm just entering my own private autumn which, at first, is a depressing realisation. I've come to love the changing colours of 'fall', but we all know that they're associated with death and decay. We all know there is a dry, lifeless brown hiding in the reds and oranges. And I'm at an age where I'm starting to see signs that the 'leaves' are 'turning', so to speak—a little greying here, a little wilting there.

And yet, while my body does what all bodies do and follows the path of entropy, my spirit has never felt stronger, my heart has never felt braver, my mind has never felt wiser. And so I'm remembering my Australian roots and learning to apply that upside-down experience to this season of life. It may be a season of decay on the outside, but inside it's spring. Easter can happen in autumn.

When jazz musician Winton Marsalis was asked, 'Why is education so important to you?' he answered, 'That's how we all experience life. Education is about our brain and our emotions and all the spiritual aspects of us. They continue to develop whereas our physicality fails us. You can lose all your physical skills and yet you can continue to read and nourish your inner self.'

While I'm sure he would have included going to school and getting a degree, I'm guessing his idea of education is much broader and includes all of life's opportunities for growth and learning, all the ways life stretches and challenges and teaches us, all the ways our hearts and minds and spirits expand while our feeble bodies shrink.

I have this quote from 2 Corinthians 4:16 beside my bathroom mirror and it restores me every time I read it:

Outwardly we are fading away but inwardly we are being renewed day by day.

That mirror never fails to remind me that, on the outside, autumn is approaching, with winter not far behind. On the outside, things are slowly dying. But there is much of me that that mirror cannot see. It can't see that, on the inside, things are growing, ideas are being born, hope is being renewed, lessons are being learned. So when winter draws to a close in my life and my body is small and grey and cold, I will have no fear, for by then, this heart will be too playful, this spirit will be too strong, this mind will be too full for such a feeble frame.

The Great Exchange

Sheridan Voysey

⁓

There are times when one must leave the safe, comfortable confines of home to learn an enduring lesson. I had an experience like that during a trip to the Central American nation of Haiti. The sights, sounds and smells will not quickly be forgotten, and neither will the lesson.

Haiti is difficult to describe. Words fail me. With 70 per cent unemployment and 80 per cent of its people living in poverty, Haiti merits its label as the most impoverished nation in the Western hemisphere. The capital city, Port-au-Prince, is the size of Sydney yet has few sealed roads. Only four-wheel drives can negotiate the rubble and pot holes, and wrecks of small cars line the streets. Electricity is irregular, as is the water supply. The landscape is barren, dusty, *grey*. Ninety-seven per cent of the trees have gone—the Spaniards and French taking all the mahogany centuries ago, and the poor today using what's left for fuel. And the houses . . . Most Haitians build their homes over years, buying a brick or two when they have the money.

Imagine your typical suburban Aussie street made entirely of incomplete, unpainted besser-brick and concrete shanty homes. That gives you an idea of what Haiti's like.

Life for Haitian children is hard. One child in fourteen never reaches their first birthday and another one in five doesn't reach the age of four. There are few public schools, and not enough teachers; only two per cent of Haitian children finish high school. I've visited seven developing countries now, and in Haiti I came across something I've seen nowhere else—children without dreams. Even children in Bangladesh aspire to become doctors or engineers or singers. Some of the Haitian kids I met desperately wanted a different life, but had no idea what that might look like.

I could go on with the sorry side of Haiti's story. But there's another, paradoxical, side. Amidst the destruction and destitution, Haiti has riches that we in developed countries like Australia know little of. In the midst of its hardship and pain, Haiti is undergoing a spiritual revival.

I was in Haiti visiting Compassion Australia projects where children are fed, clothed, and given healthcare and education through the sponsorship of people like you and me. Compassion programs are run by local churches, and all the churches we visited had no fewer than 1000 members each. Haitian Christians 'pray-in' every single meal and are thankful for whatever God provides (even if it's one potato shared among the whole family late at night). Even the most conservative churches run deliverance services and see Haitians released from demonic spirits and spells. The faith of the Haitians is passionate, persevering and powerful. As one pastor told me, 'In Haiti, every day is a physical and spiritual battle. You simply cannot win that battle without Jesus.'

On the plane flight home from Haiti I flicked through one of the magazines in the seat pocket in front of me. It was one of those Sky Mall brochures, full of things to purchase through the airline. Oh, the things you could buy! 'Gravity-defying shoes' with a spring-loaded heel to give you bounce; a mini-microwave for your desk, saving that laborious walk to the kitchen to reheat your coffee. There was a luxury mattress in there for your dog, and a portable foot spa in there for you. You could even buy full-size '80s-style arcade games, and mini Automatic Teller Machines that doled out money to your kids.

I read, and I winced.

Because while we buy luxury beds for our pooches, Haitian children sleep on cold cement floors. And while we fill our empty lives with trinkets, Haitian Christians are meeting God in profound ways. It was then that I realised the developing world needs our generosity and we in Australia need the developing world's faith. We have what they want, and they have what we need.

A great exchange needs to take place—we give up the consumer toys for the sake of the poor, so that we might catch the faith that makes them so rich.

Air Rage

Scott Wegener

～

Should a plane I'm in lose its wings and start to plummet to earth, I'd probably exclaim, 'Wow, this is much better than "zooming" on Google Earth!'

Because of my love of aerial photos, the opportunity to fly always brings an un-normal urgency to secure a window seat. One time, this urge brought out an uglier side of me I didn't know existed.

I'd arrived at the airport more than two hours before take-off and was delighted at the thought of getting a guaranteed window seat. As I checked in at the computer kiosk, I noticed I was in seat 39J. *Hallelujah, a window seat,* I thought and proceeded to do an imaginary hula dance while I waited for my boarding pass to be printed.

I was hoping the plane would approach for landing over our house this time. I'd seen plenty fly over but I wanted to be able to look down at what I would look like, looking up at people looking down.

As the flight started boarding I quickly joined the queue, wanting to make sure no one accidentally sat in my window seat first.

As I wandered up the aisle, it took extra brain power to find my seat due to the sea of vacancies.

'37 ... 38 ... 39! ... or is this 38?' I always have trouble lining up the row numbers with the corresponding seats.

I went on one more row and found that row 40 was just before an emergency exit. I momentarily pondered about the view if we could travel with the door open, then turned to sit in my seat, 39J.

WHOOSH! In darts a lady who takes a dive for the window seat. Slightly amused by her mistake, I pulled out my ticket and, with my best 'I'm lost in a foreign country' look, asked, 'Is this row 39?'

She abruptly returned fire with 'yes'.

Not one who likes conflict, I decided to humbly sacrifice my window view for the opportunity to get my elbow bumped by every service cart that travelled the aisle.

After watching the safety demonstration, when I'd normally practise looking out the window for the flight ahead, I was a little disappointed they didn't ask for a show of hands of who thought they were meant to be in a window seat.

I glanced over and saw this woman had her head buried in a book. 'Oh, that's just swell,' I thought. 'She's not even looking out the window.'

I kind of hoped she would need to go to the toilet, as I'd planned quite a fuss when she tried to squeeze past. In the meantime, I was making every effort to look out the window over her, in the hope of an offer to swap places.

About halfway through the flight, and exhausted from stretching my neck, I conceded defeat.

I put my seat back and just stared at the roof, the little voice in my head muttering away at how I was the one who should have been seated at the window. *I'm Mr 39J and here on the roof it's clearly labelled 39J—Aisle, 39K—Window . . .* The voice in my head went silent for a moment as the realisation hit. I'd been sitting in my designated seat all along.

I spent the rest of the flight muttering to myself about what a fool I'd been, and how I'd been judging this poor lady all this time and heaping bitter thoughts upon her.

Normally I pride myself on giving people the benefit of the doubt. People can cut in front of me in their car and I'll assume they are heading to the hospital to see their dying mother. A waiter can give the poorest service in the world and I'll assume they've been evicted from their rental that morning.

But here, in one moment of my own error, I had lost any claim to 'being joyful always' and succumbed to negativity.

There was one positive, however. At least the plane didn't crash while I was stuck in an aisle seat. Then I would have been really upset with my viewless seat allocation!

Floating Mercy

Amos Bennett

❧

'I think the work being done by volunteers with Mercy Ships is giving the people hope.' That is how Townsville nurse Amy Cassidy sums summed up her experience among 450 volunteers from around the world on the world's largest private hospital ship in West Africa.

The *Africa Mercy* was on a ten-month assignment to Liberia, one of the world's poorest nations. It was the third such visit to Liberia in three years and the fourth since the United Nations first invited Mercy Ships to visit Liberia in 2005, prior to the country's free elections ending fourteen years of civil war.

For ten weeks in 2008 Amy worked as a ward nurse, caring for post-operative patients recovering from free surgery for a range of conditions related to disability and disfigurement, as well as women recovering from surgery to correct obstetric fistula problems.

'As I walked down the streets of the capital Monrovia I rarely saw people smiling,' she said. 'There were very obvious signs of poverty, a lack of social welfare, an inconsistent system of justice, and a general lack of happiness among the people, who had suffered so much from a very long and hurtful war. It is easy to read of such things and see the images on television. In some ways it is just the way we have seen it, but when you are there it is almost surreal in many ways.

'After ten weeks working among the people of Liberia I felt more a part of their lives and their struggles. It was great to be able to interact with the people, to make them smile and to encourage them that there is a God who is big and who cares for them.'

Amy first learnt of the work of Mercy Ships through Google when she started her nurse training.

'It seemed then to be the perfect opportunity to share my experiences, and to bring a challenge to me through such an experience. During my training I had some great opportunities to try my hand at a variety of aspects of nursing. That meant that I did at least have some form of familiarity with the different operations performed by the volunteer surgeons onboard. Another thing that also helped me to adapt to living in close quarters with others from about forty different nationalities came from my growing up and moving around different environments.

'The reaction from some of my friends to my decision to offer myself as a volunteer was interesting. Some were intrigued and could not understand why I would be willing to pay my own way to go and work in Africa. Other friends and family were very supportive and keen to hear of my experiences.'

Getting from Townsville to Liberia was quite an experience in itself. 'I finished work one day and drove north to Cairns and stayed there with friends. The following day I flew to Brisbane, then on to Hong Kong. After a four-hour stopover, I boarded another eight-hour flight to Qatar, with another short break and on to Dubai. I spent seventeen hours in Dubai before catching my five-hour flight to Nairobi, for the five-hour leg to Monrovia with a stopover in Accra, Ghana. In all, it took about three days of constant travel.'

There were many highlights during the ten weeks on the hospital ship, Amy says. 'One was working with a patient who had his leg amputated below the knee. I was able to spend time giving him encouragement. It was frustrating to hear his story and to know that I was limited in what I could offer him, due purely to the lack of resources. But it was great to share some words with him.

'I also grabbed a picture from the internet of a disabled Olympian, to try and encourage him to forget what was behind and press onwards towards a better future. He was amazed when he saw the picture of someone running on prosthetic legs. It was never tiring to see him smile. I just hope he can keep on smiling in the hard months and years to come.'

Looking back on her time away, Amy says that the best thing was the decision to do it. 'It was great to actually go to Liberia and experience this place for myself. The worst decision was probably forgetting to pack some Vegemite to eat at breakfast. But I did manage to get hold of some from other Aussies onboard!'

Mercy Ships is an international Christian charity that has operated hospital ships in developing nations since 1978. <www.mercyships. org.au>

Three Lessons in Humility

Charles Widdowson

~

The 'bus' slowly chugged its way up the mountain from Baguio City to Kapangan, a rural municipality in Benguet province in the northern Philippines.

My travelling companion and host, Andrew Sacuy-Ap, sat beside me and reassured his far-from-comfortable guest that all was well. The 'bus', he told me, had been in service twice a day since the war and had only had minor break-downs. I noticed, however, he didn't stipulate which war, and I refrained from asking.

The track on which we were travelling was only just as wide as the bus. Our seats were on the left side and the view was of a steep drop of some 200 metres.

'What happens,' I asked Andrew, 'if we meet a vehicle coming the other way, or something happens to this—er—vehicle?'

He looked at me and smiled.

'Then Charles, you should be praying even harder than you are now. However, it is most unlikely. You see, there is no motorised transport in Kapangan.'

'None at all?'

'None whatsoever.'

'Then how do all the folk get about? How do they travel to church?'

'They walk, Charles. And just bear in mind that some families live miles from the church and may well be walking for two or three hours.' He paused and then added, 'Each way.'

'So how many will be attending church tomorrow?' I asked.

Andrew pursed his lips and put his head on one side. 'Oh! There'll be a meeting tonight and you can expect maybe two hundred.'

As I was taking all this in, the 'bus' lurched and stopped. I hung on to the seat in front for grim death, not daring to look at the steep drop down.

As I was about to express my concern, Andrew's calm voice reassured me.

'Don't worry, it happens now and then. It's probably only gear box trouble and it's probably happened before.'

Slowly he made his way over the sacks and bags that were obstructing the gangway, handing off the occasional dog, pig or cockerel, until he reached the front of the 'bus'. From the door he was able to chat with the driver and, looking pleased, he made his way back to me.

'Just as I thought,' he told me, 'a bit of trouble with the gear box. Easily fixed with a rubber band, so we'll be on our way shortly.'

Eventually, with no further mishaps, after a three-hour journey (to cover roughly 35 kilometres) we arrived at our destination—and what a destination!

Andrew and I stepped into Shangri-La.

As soon as we descended from the 'bus' we were surrounded by a group of exuberant youngsters singing, 'I am redeemed by the blood of the Lamb', men and women wanting to greet the 'Australian Reverend' and, in their midst, Gavino Doang, their minister. All pressed in to welcome me by hugging me and loving me and telling me how welcome I was and how excited they were.

Totally overwhelmed, I did my best to hug and love in return.

I must admit that from the moment Andrew had mentioned visiting Kapangan, I had had doubts. These had increased when I saw the deprivation of the people and the state of the 'bus', and they certainly weren't helped by the break-down. But now, phew! I felt utterly and completely humbled.

Somehow Gavino rescued Andrew and me from the singing, shouting, praising welcomers and led us—with all of them following—to his home, pointing out the church as we passed.

I looked around and was amazed to see that this whole area was as flat as a pancake, and mentioned this to Gavino. 'Ah!' he smiled. 'During the last war the Americans used this as an air-base. They literally sliced the top off this mountain, and when the war was over they gave it to the church.'

I was shaking my head, more and more amazed at the incredible way Father God works.

Soon the 'praisers' had left and Andrew and I were ushered into Gavino's home, where we met his wife, Emily, and his seven children.

'Bring your case upstairs,' he told me. I followed and soon found myself in a small, bare room. There was a window with a bamboo 'curtain' and a trestle made from narra wood, hard and black. 'Come down when you're ready,' he told me, and left.

'Excuse me, Gavino,' I called after him. 'Where's the bathroom so that I can freshen up?'

'I am so sorry,' he called back, 'we don't have any bathrooms upstairs. Come down and I'll show you.'

I did. He took me outside the house where there was a bucket of cold water.

'This is what you would call the "bathroom".'

'But . . .'

'I know.' His face broke into a broad grin. 'Here we have no running water, no gas and no electricity. This bucket is your basin and . . .'—he turned and indicated the bushes—'that is your toilet. Enjoy your "freshening up",' he told me and went off chuckling to himself.

I was assuredly 'back to nature'.

After a simple meal of rice and bananas ('I grow fifteen varieties of bananas up here,' Gavino said proudly) we went into the church for pre-meeting prayer.

There were about one hundred people in church and Andrew whispered in my ear: 'Sorry, I was wrong.' However, they sounded more like three hundred as they sang out their praises to God, led by Emily and an absolutely gorgeous choir of youngsters.

Andrew introduced me, and through Gavino I gave my testimony, followed by a challenge to accept Jesus as Saviour. Seven responded and there was a clapping and shouting as the folk, who of course knew all seven, welcomed them into God's kingdom. We finished with prayers for healing and thirty responded, many of whom testified to immediate results. This, again, was received with tumultuous praise.

It was, indeed, a night to remember.

My only concern as I wearily made my way upstairs was this: how was I going to sleep on a slab of narra wood? However, I was too tired to worry, and using my rolled-up trousers as a pillow, I lowered myself gently on the wooden bed.

It was as I lay there, thanking Jesus for such a precious evening, that a miracle occurred. No longer was I lying on a wooden slab. It was as if there was a mattress of clouds under me and I slept like a baby.

I awoke fresh and ready for whatever the next day held, and it held a lot.

The nine o'clock service lasted for about two hours and was more or less along the same lines as the night before, except that it included communion. There was, however, no place for a message, which surprised me, especially as I had been asked to prepare one.

I looked at Andrew and lifted my hands and shoulders in a questioning attitude, but he only smiled and mouthed, 'It's OK.'

The service finished and drinks of tea or water were handed round.

At about 11.30 am we all trooped back into church and I was asked to bring the message God had given to me. They said they'd like it to last about an hour or so. So I shared from my heart on 1 John 3:1, 'How great is the love the Father has lavished on us', and spoke on the charismatic power to love.

Lunch—more rice and bananas—followed, and at about two o'clock Gavino clapped his hands and motioned everybody to sit round him on the ground.

'This afternoon,' he announced, 'we are going to open the meeting so you can ask Charles to answer any questions you may want to. Let's give him another Kapangan welcome.'

To shouts and cheers I stood and explained that I might not have all the answers. To which Gavino replied, 'If Charles cannot answer your question, he will show you which passage of scripture *will* answer it.'

I wished I had just kept quiet. But God looked after everything and it went well.

At almost five o'clock Gavino announced that it was only just over an hour to the evening meeting and tea would be served. (There was no need to ask what it was!) During the break I took Gavino aside and told him how very thrilled I was that he had organised the day as he had.

'What do you mean?' he asked.

'Well,' I replied, 'the morning meeting without the message, so that I had plenty of time to preach. Then the time of questions and answers this afternoon. It's so kind of you.'

A look of astonishment appeared on Gavino's face.

'This is Kapangan, Charles,' he explained. 'This is what we normally do. Please don't think for a minute it's been laid on just for you. It's our normal way of spending Sunday. Some of these dear folk will leave home early Sunday morning, spend their day worshipping and praising God, learning from his Word and enjoying fellowship with each other. Then, after the evening service, they will walk back home, arriving late in the night.'

'Every Sunday?' I queried.

'Why not?' Gavino said simply. 'It's God's day and we give it all to him. However,' he added, 'because *you* are here everybody has decided to take a holiday tomorrow and we're going to do it all again.'

For the second time I felt so humble as I thought of my own attitude towards Sunday—and that of so many others, not only in Australia but around the world.

After the evening service that night I lay down on my narra bed and sank, once again, into God's cloud of love.

Monday followed the same pattern as Sunday and ended with us all praying for Andrew and Gavino as I laid hands on them. I also had some prophetic words for the dear Kapangan folk.

My third humbling came on the Tuesday morning as Gavino, Andrew, myself and some people who lived nearby waited for the 'bus' to take us back to Baguio City. Gavino took me to one side and put his arm round my shoulder.

'Dear brother,' he said, 'last night I hardly slept. I spent most of it on my knees thanking God for sending you to us, and as I was kneeling there before him, he told me to give you my most treasured possession.'

I was overwhelmed. Here was a man who received the equivalent of $A49.00 a month. With this he had to feed and clothe his family and pay for his children's schooling. What could it be that he treasured most?

'When I was first converted to Christ,' he told me, 'I walked these hills preaching the gospel as a travelling evangelist. I carried my Bible in the sack my forebears had used to carry the heads of their victims. It was hard going, but in time God blessed me with converts. My very first convert gave me a cross. It is very simple, just two pieces of hard, rough narra wood joined together. I've worn it round my neck ever since, and as I read my Bible I stroke my cross. I want you to have it.'

From his pocket he took a smooth, shiny cross hanging from a leather strap. Taking my hand, he opened it and placed his cross in my palm. He then closed my fingers over it.

'There,' he smiled, 'now it's yours.'

I could only hug him, and tears were in my eyes as I thanked him.

At that moment our transport arrived and Andrew and I scrambled aboard. I was not the only one who felt emotional as the 'bus' chugged away.

Now that cross, the symbol of our redemption, is my most treasured possession.

Mexican Encounter

Nola Passmore

~

It was hot and humid, the air so thick we got puffed just walking around. Our heavy black tracksuit pants didn't help. Every movement was an effort. We were about to do our first street performance in Mexico.

It had been organised by a group of Christian women called Mujer de Éxito, which loosely translated means 'successful woman' or 'woman of triumph'. The women had been praying for their neighbourhood in Guadalajara for years and were excited about the visiting drama team from Youth With A Mission (YWAM). My first thought was that they didn't look very Mexican. They were middle class, most didn't have dark hair, and there wasn't a sombrero in sight. I guess my naive view had been based on too many bad westerns.

Our stage was the cement surface of a dead-end street. A set of stairs stretching the full width of the street served as seats for our audience, though two workmen also watched from a rooftop. The roofs were all flat in that area, with some holding washing lines laden with clothes. It was an interesting backdrop.

José, the director of the YWAM base, was working with us that day. Four of the drama team members began by doing a short, amusing piece called 'The Chair', which was often performed to draw a crowd. Then one of the team members gave her testimony while José translated the visitor's English into Spanish.

Next it was my turn. I played a demon-like creature called a 'maggot' in our major drama, 'Encounter', a seventeen-minute piece performed with mime and dance to a musical soundtrack. It began with God creating the world, represented by a girl called 'Creation'. God and Creation were in perfect harmony until a group of five maggots, who had been lying dormant by the side of the stage, awoke and enticed Creation away with drugs, pride, money and other worldly pursuits.

Since I was deemed to have rhythm, I was the first maggot to arise from our sinister huddle. From my place at the front of the stage, my movements had to keep the beat for the rest of the maggots. My big moment each performance came when I injected Creation with drugs (or more correctly, lunged at her with an empty plastic syringe!).

As the maggots lured Creation away from God, she took off her white gloves and the maggots replaced them with black ones. The maggots also took strips of black cloth representing bondages from around their necks and placed them on

Creation one by one. Creation eventually wanted to remove the bondages, but she couldn't in her own strength. God then came forward, took the bondages from her and put them around his own neck. The maggots mocked him as he died during the crucifixion scene, which was all done in dramatic slow motion. Then, with a loud burst of music, God came back to life, broke the bondages and defeated the maggots. We crashed to the ground and lay there for the last couple of minutes while God and Creation were reconciled. When God took off Creation's black gloves and replaced them with white ones again, there were usually tears in the eyes of onlookers. I loved performing it.

As soon as it was finished, we went to a nearby house to change. The vigorous performance and the heat had left us exhausted and all we could think about was getting some water. Next minute, one of the team members came running and said, 'Quick, you've gotta see this.' I moved back out to the street to see what was happening. José had given a short message and an altar call, and every single person in the audience of 40 or 50 came forward for prayer—men and women, old people and children, all wanting to give their lives to Christ. We had seen some people touched by our performances in San Diego earlier that month, but nothing like this. I was suddenly overwhelmed by the goodness of God and felt tears streaming down my face as I ran to join in prayers for the group. We couldn't understand the words because they were all in Spanish, but we could see what God was doing. The women from Mujer de Éxito were so excited and quickly went round getting names and contact details so they could follow up the people.

That night, the women invited us to a special meal in our honour, but we knew the responsiveness of the people had little to do with us. It had everything to do with the women's prayers, their faithfulness, the work of the Holy Spirit, and the faithfulness of our Lord in drawing people to himself. While we had a good response almost everywhere we went in Mexico, we never again had an occasion where the entire audience came forward. I think that was God's special blessing to us as well.

Though I haven't performed Encounter since that ten-week outreach in 1994, I've never forgotten that encounter with God. Sometimes when I'm sitting in my conservative clothes at my conservative desk at my conservative job, a little part of me wishes I could don that maggot outfit and do a little jig in the corridor. Maybe tomorrow.

Opportunity Maker

Nathan Brown

David Bussau, advocate for the world's poor and co-founder of global microfinance company Opportunity International, sums up his contribution to society simply: 'God created me to be an entrepreneur, and I realised that the best thing I had to contribute to society was those entrepreneurial skills. The problem is the poor have never had the assets to be able to go to the commercial sources of finance and, in fact, they don't even have the sandals on their feet to be able to get in the door of the bank.'

For David, his recognition as Senior Australian of the Year on Australia Day 2008 was more a platform for continuing to speak for the poor than a crowning recognition of lifelong achievement—it was another opportunity to serve others.

David never knew his parents. Before he was old enough to have any clear memories, he was abandoned at an orphanage in Masterton, New Zealand.

It became the only childhood home he knew. He has said

149

that one of his primary motivations for a life spent in giving to others is that he does not want any other child to go through what he did growing up.

When he was fifteen, the orphanage found him a job and a place at a boarding house—and he was on his own.

Determined to be able to make his own decisions in life, David applied his entrepreneurial flair and hard work to doing so, beginning with a single hotdog stand outside a football stadium that, within a few months, grew to half a dozen such stands. A fish and chip shop and a hamburger bar followed, and in his late twenties, now married, he moved to Australia and began working in the construction industry.

'Even though I didn't have knowledge or experience about construction, I think I had the tenacity and aggressiveness to have a go at it,' he told ABC TV's *Australian Story*. 'From there, within a short period of time, and using my own capital, I bought into the construction company and then bought out the partner, then set up other construction companies to complement that program.'

By age thirty-five, David was a millionaire and seemingly in charge of his destiny.

But questions came with success. 'We really felt we had been challenged to look at our lifestyle, assess what we were doing with our lives and what we were doing with what we had,' he recalls. 'We had to reconsider where we put our energies and where we put our resources.

'We had reached a point where we recognised the economics of enough. We had enough to live on for the rest of our life so we turned our attention to setting up a family trust. This trust was the seed for Opportunity International.'

But his story was a little more complicated than that. Moved by the Cyclone Tracy's destruction of Darwin on Christmas Day, 1974, David organised a team of tradesmen from his company to assist with clean-up and rebuilding. With his family, which now included two young daughters, he moved to Darwin to lend a hand.

Then, in 1976, a major earthquake hit Bali, Indonesia, destroying villages and infrastructure. Again, David and his family moved in response to disaster.

'Of course it was strange to start off with,' he begins retelling the story. 'We couldn't even speak the language. But it was the beginning of a journey and a whole new season of life, where we learned to understand and appreciate the poor and see the beauty of the poor, rather than pitying them.

'The village was remote—it was a 14-kilometre walk from the nearest road—and there was no electricity or telephones, toilets or running water. For our kids, it was a wonderful time. They look back on it and reminisce about the great time they had living in the village.

'But for me, one of the salient points to come out of this was to be able to relate to people who have nothing. It can be difficult for us in the West—we have so much stuff around us we don't know what it's like to have nothing—to go into someone's home and see that the only piece of furniture they have is a chair and to see the simplicity of their lifestyle.

'What that did to Carol and me was to enable us to see the depravity in our own life, which was cluttered with possessions, ambitions and self-interest. So the poor have really been instrumental in setting me off on a whole new journey, which I have been travelling for thirty years.'

It was here that David stumbled across the idea of micro-finance, a concept he pioneered which has transformed the approach to combating poverty around the world. 'We were building a dam and Ketut, the foreman, was sharing with me one day that he and his wife were about to have their fourth baby,' he says. 'But while the baby was still inside the womb, he or she would inherit four generations of debt. Ketut was worried the next generation was going to continue to suffer this indebtedness to loan sharks, who would continue to take 60 per cent of their harvest in payment of the debt.

'He asked me what suggestions I had for how his family might be able to get out of this situation. And I asked him a simple question: what gifts and talents do you have?

'He said, "My wife is very good at sewing." So I said, "I tell you what: I'll loan you some money. I'll lend you $100 and you buy a sewing machine, make products and take them to the market. And when you make money you can pay me back and I will charge you just a little bit of interest." '

It was an appropriate entrepreneurial response to the situation but had some immediate implications. 'We were very aware that if we just gave him a gift then everyone else in the village would also want $100,' David explains. 'And we really wanted him to have the dignity of being able to repay it.'

It was the beginning of something big. For Ketut and his family, it was the end of poverty—they now export furniture, own a fleet of taxis and employ a number of people from their village. For David, the idea of microfinance had sprouted. He set up a family trust to begin to implement this concept on a wider scale which, in conjunction with US businessman Al Whittaker, in 1979 grew into Opportunity International.

'When we started this thirty years ago, we were ostracised and even despised by the development set, by the "good guys" who were alleviating poverty,' David says. 'Most of them had the "Robin Hood" approach of taking from the rich and giving to the poor—and then the rich keep getting it back from the poor.

'The prevailing paradigm thirty years ago—and, in some places, still today—is that the resources of the world are small and we need to find how to cut the cake so everyone has a slice. But for me, the question was not "why is the cake so small?" but "why don't we make a bigger cake and then more people can have a piece of it?"

'So the basis was the biblical concept of enabling people to create wealth so they can enjoy the riches of the earth. Not enabling them to be dependent on others but to live with the dignity of providing for themselves.'

Today, Opportunity International is a worldwide development organisation that has given 1.25 million small loans to people in twenty-three countries. Their work creates a job in the developing world every thirty seconds and they estimate that every permanent job created directly lifts six people out of poverty.

The numbers are impressive, but the stories David is first to tell are of families and communities strengthened in ways that are not just economic—mothers (84 per cent of these loans are made to women) with confidence to rebuild their lives and hope that their children will not have to overcome the poverty that has bound them.

'Then there's the other end of the spectrum,' he adds. 'One of our clients was a woman who used to sell onions on the side of the road. She received a small loan from us and—to cut a long story short—is now a conglomerate. She floated the company last year and now has 2300 employees.'

So, now a sixty-nine year old 'senior Australian', what keeps David working and travelling as much as he does for a variety of projects and causes?

'I think a lot of it is self-centredness—I enjoy the challenge,' he says. 'But I think deep down in my spirit there is a need to respond to my destiny, the purpose for which I was put on the planet. God gifted me to do this.

'My perception of God is probably screwed up a bit. But my perception of God is [that he is] like an investment banker—and he expects a return on his investment. In fact, the Bible says he wants a hundredfold return on the investment, not just 10 per cent.

'God has poured so many blessings into my life and my family, so he has given me a responsibility to give that return on investment. This keeps driving me to seek how I can be used to contribute to God's kingdom.'

Opportunity International's web address is <www.opportunity. org.au>.

The Miner's Lamp

Gordon Moyes

~

We have few antiques in our home, and those we have came down through our families. But since both sides were working people on limited incomes, they never had anything of great value. The small things we do have rest on the shelves of book cases in front of the ranks of books. Visitors pick them up and look at them with interest.

One item is a small brass lamp once used on a miner's helmet. I got it from Broken Hill, but it was originally used in Moonta. It is ten centimetres high with a reflector eight centimetres across made of highly polished silver. It has a hook on the back that clipped into the miner's helmet. The bottom unscrews, and into the compartment was placed crushed calcium carbide rock. In the top half of the lamp is a screw top hole through which water was poured. A control allowed a steady drip of water onto the rock, which produced acetylene gas. Another control allowed a steady stream of gas to come out of a nozzle in the centre of the reflector. This gas is combustible, and when lit gave a steady flame.

The jet where the gas was ignited had to be cleared by using a fine wire 'pricker'. The lamp was shaken to get the gas generation going and then the stream of gas coming from the jet was lit with a match. Care was required as explosions could occur. These lamps with their tiny flame are outlawed in mines today, but for a century they provided the only light in the pitch black mine shafts.

Moonta is one of the South Australian towns that form the Yorke Peninsula's famous Copper Triangle. Today the population falls well short of the peak of 12,000 in 1875 when huge tonnages of copper ore were mined.

Today the grand old buildings financed by mining wealth make Moonta one of the state's most valuable heritage assets. The Triangle is also known as 'Little Cornwall' and the community's indebtedness to the many Cornishmen who crossed the world to work the mines is celebrated in May of every odd-numbered year with the Kernewek Lowender festival. Today the Old Sweet Shop introduces children to traditional humbugs and the like, while their parents can chomp into a Cornish pastie.

When Matthew Flinders passed along the coast near the present-day site of Moonta in 1802, the region was inhabited by the Narrungga people. Moonta takes its name from a Narrungga word meaning 'place of impenetrable scrub'.

Copper was discovered at Moonta in 1861 and the mine prospered. A history of the Moonta Company written in 1914 records: 'during its existence [it] produced £5,396,146 worth of copper, and distributed £1,168,000 among shareholders. It had the distinction of being the first mining company in Australia to pay over £1,000,000 in dividends.'

In order to attract miners to the area an advertisement was circulated in England: 'Free. Emigration to Port Adelaide, South Australia. Married agricultural laborers, shepherds, blacksmiths, wheelwrights, employers, tailors, shoe-makers, brick-makers, builders and all persons engaged in useful occupations may obtain a free passage to South Australia where they are within the regulations of the Colonial Commissioners.'

The first miners at Moonta were Cornishmen, using methods developed in Cornwall over several centuries. The lodes were rich and ore could be seen by candlelight. By 1875 Moonta was the second-largest town in South Australia.

In 1980 I studied with Professor J. Edwin Orr, then the greatest historian of evangelical religious revivals in the world. He alerted me to a revival in the mines at Moonta. Standing at one point in Moonta, a visitor could have seen nineteen churches and chapels.

From the early 1860s, Cornish culture and religion dominated the area for sixty years. Cornish religion was Methodist, Wesleyan Methodist, Primitive Methodist and Bible Christian—and Cornish Methodism meant frequent revivals, of which that in 1875 was the most remarkable.

Historian Stuart Piggin describes the events involved.

'Three deaths seem to have been the sparks which ignited the fires of this revival. On 15 March 1875, Hugh Datson, a mine manager or "captain", was fatally injured in a rock fall at Moonta. He had been brought to saving faith in Christ through the preaching of an evangelist from Yorkshire. Datson had been a model Wesleyan, never failing in his attendance at class meetings and prayer meetings. He would pray to the point of exhaustion for the conversion of sinners. For a week after his funeral, services were held daily in the Wesleyan church and a number of conversions were reported.

'Then the action switched to the Bible Christian church at Moonta. On Sunday evening, 4 April, a funeral service was held for Kate Morcombe, a young woman from the Sunday school. In the prayer meeting following the sermon, fifteen souls, affected by the early death of a much-loved friend, were won for Christ. Meetings were held daily in the ensuing week and a further forty-five were converted. Then on Sunday 11 April the evening prayer meeting was accompanied by cries for mercy and much distress and the determination to break the chains of Satan and flee to Christ. Forty more were added to the church. A circus was in town that day, but no one was interested in attending. Much greater excitement was to be found in church. The circus left the next day.

'Revival returned to the Wesleyan church the following Sunday, 18 April, when the death of a third person was the focus of the service, and in the ensuing week ninety more

159

claimed to have found forgiveness through Christ. Most of the converts were men and women aged between sixteen and twenty-five. In the same week a further sixty came to Christ in other Wesleyan churches in Little Cornwall.

'By Sunday 25 April the river of life was flowing freely, and "the penitents were seeking salvation from early morning to late at night". By now the congregation at the Primitive Methodist Church was experiencing the same blessing. By 9 May, 198 new members had been added to the Bible Christian church, doubling its membership. The revival river was still flowing in Moonta a year later. The number of conversions in all the churches was estimated by the Bible Christians to be 1250 and by the Wesleyans to be 1550.'

According to the 1891 census, 80 per cent of Little Cornwall's population claimed to be Methodist. Between them the Wesleyans, Primitive Methodists and Bible Christians built at least thirty-one churches in the area. The largest, the Wesleyan church at the nearby settlement of Moonta Mines, could seat 1200, and still stands today.

'The congregations were not wealthy,' Piggin continues. 'Employment in the mines was episodic, subject to downturns and booms, and in the low times the miners struggled to make a subsistence wage. But there were wealthy Wesleyans, those who had learned well from John Wesley how to make the best of both worlds, and who heeded his advice not only to make all they could and save all they could, but also to give all they could.'

Piggin tells the story of a Methodist lay leader named Henry Richard Hancock. Hancock was the 'captain' (superintendent) of both the mine at Moonta and another at Wallaroo, eighteen kilometres to the north. On Sundays he was the superintendent of the Wesleyan Sunday school, which, with over six hundred members, was the largest in the colony for thirty years.

'He once called the entire mining community together— about 1500 of them—and shared with them that the mine was in peril because of a downturn in trade. Expecting to hear the bad news of numerous retrenchments, they heard him instead outline his visionary plans for expansion and putting on more staff so that new ore bodies could be opened up, which would lower the average cost of production and therefore make their product more saleable. They were aware that their destiny was in his hands and they knew how to defer to him. When Captain Hancock and his family entered the church, it is said that the congregation stood out of respect . . . [But] Captain Hancock's attempts at preaching were not acceptable to them because he could not preach extempore sermons. His habit of writing out his sermons beforehand and reading them was dismissed as "Not fitty!" '

According to Piggin, the richly emotional expressions of faith in Little Cornwall were appropriate to the hard lives of the mining communities.

'The life of a miner was always at risk through danger of accidents and the slow death of inhaled dust. It was also hard and tedious work. Methodism offered dramatic relief with the wholehearted singing of its choirs and congregations and the fervent oratory of its preachers. It offered fun and laughter: church services were not dour affairs, and preachers, who were expected to preach for fifty minutes without notes, did not have to be educated, but they had to be enthusiastic and entertaining.

'In 1874, the year before the great Moonta revival, the miners went on strike and then formed the Moonta Miners Association. The leaders of this trade union were Methodist local preachers. They were not Marxist revolutionaries. They wanted social justice without socialism. Their Methodism was displayed by their call for prohibition and by their holding a service of thanksgiving at the end of the strike.

'The most celebrated of Little Cornwall's Methodist politicians was "Honest John" Verran. He was a Primitive Methodist local preacher with a reputation for charismatic oratory. He was elected to parliament in 1901 and was Labor Premier of South Australia from 1910 to 1912. On becoming premier, he travelled to Moonta, and to a crowd of 2000 he gave credit where it was due by announcing that he was an MP because he was a PM (Primitive Methodist). From all parts of the crowd came cries of "Amen" and "Glory".'

My little miner's lamp was worn by a Moonta miner, probably a Cornishman, probably a Methodist. I wonder if he was part of that revival?

What to Boast In

Nicole Starling

~~~

*Y*esterday I woke up tired and in a bad mood (after having been woken up numerous times during the night by all three children). I walked up to drop the kids at school/preschool (in the rain) and got home (wet) to receive an email from the mother of a friend I studied law with. The mother was letting me know about my friend's promotion. A *really* good promotion, impressively described in the press release that she'd attached to the email.

My first reaction was to feel a pang of jealousy. Then defensiveness. Sometimes I hate the fact that I look like a fool to my fellow law graduates because of some of the decisions I've made (marrying a pastor in my last year at uni was only the start in a sad tale of downward mobility). I hate those moments when I see myself as they must see me—a woman who has thrown her career away, looking every bit the stay-at-home mum, living in suburbia, about to go out and do the grocery shopping for the week.

163

Then my pride *really* kicked in as I reminded myself of all the reasons why I had made *better* decisions than her, how *I* should be congratulated for staying at home with my little ones, of all the hours of 'quality time' I had spent with them, how they'll be so well adjusted when they grow up . . . (I think you get the drift).

It wasn't until later in the day that I remembered Galatians 6:14 (NASB):

But may it never be that I would boast, except in the cross of our Lord Jesus Christ, through which the world has been crucified to me, and I to the world.

I had been boasting in *myself* and not in the cross. Even decisions that *are* good decisions aren't about me, but about Jesus. I'm glad that I'm able to be at home with my kids at this stage of their lives, but it won't have a skerrick of eternal significance if my life doesn't point them to Jesus. And it won't point them to Jesus if I'm too busy congratulating myself on all my 'good decisions'.

If the world really has been 'crucified' to me, then I don't need to answer its boasts with defensive, worldly 'boasting' of my own. Much, much better to boast in Jesus than in my stay-at-homeness!

Winning the Marathon

Barry Chant

❧

Every year at Wesley International Congregation, Sydney, 'Thank You Lord Sunday' is a special event. On that occasion, a special offering is collected as an expression of our thanks to God for his goodness and love towards us.

When I first accepted the position of Senior Pastor, the total given was in the vicinity of $30,000. Within twelve months we had set a target of $40,000. It took us two years to reach it, but we did. So we lifted the goal to $50,000.

If I remember rightly, I set this target myself without actually consulting anyone. I announced it on Sunday morning hoping that no one would object to my unilateral action. No one did.

Not that anyone was likely to be upset about it. The elders could hardly complain if the offering increased. And if it didn't, we were no worse off—unless, of course, the offering went down as a protest against my asking for too much.

But all was well. We didn't actually reach the target but we raised more than we had done previously—well over forty thousand.

So the next year, 2007, I proposed a $50,000 goal again. During the week, one of our members suggested I was aiming too low. 'What's wrong with setting a target of $100,000?' he asked.

It was all right for him—he didn't have to face the people. But when I stood on the platform that Sunday morning, I found myself saying, 'Our target today once again is $50,000. But it has been suggested to me that we should go for double that amount. Could we believe God for $100,000?'

We have a bright, lively multicultural congregation of over a thousand people, mainly of Asian origin, although all English-speaking. They have always been generous, but possibly because of their Asian heritage, they also tend to be astute with their handling of their finances, and reluctant to waste money. When they give, they do so thoughtfully.

As it happened, the brother who suggested doubling our expectation put in $50,000 himself! And our total offering was $95,000.

The following year, I decided to preach more openly on giving. Two Sunday services were planned for this and the date was set. But then we had the opportunity to include two missionary speakers in our program and this meant re-scheduling. Easy enough.

But a week before 'Thank You Lord Sunday', trouble emerged.

Every year in Sydney, there is a Sunday marathon race in which tens of thousands of runners participate. It's a great event and it draws international interest. But it also means that the CBD is largely closed off to anyone else. As Wesley Mission is located right in the middle of the city, this always creates problems for us.

A week before 'Thank You Lord Sunday', I learned that we had programmed it for the day of the marathon. People were going to find it hard to get to church. We examined our program, but we found that to shift it now would create significant difficulties and clashes with other long-planned events. We decided there was no choice but to proceed.

So I went ahead and preached on first fruits—the Old Testament concept of giving the first of the flock or the herd or the crop to God; and on tithing—systematic, sacrificial and honest giving to the Lord. I also told them how in Scripture offerings were for two main purposes: to support the ministry and to care for the poor. Wesley International Congregation was doing both as the previous financial year we had given $200,000 to overseas missions and $300,000 to the work of Wesley Mission with the poor and needy. We wanted to do even better this year.

The next weekend, on the Saturday night, I downloaded a map of the marathon route. It was worse than I thought. The whole city was encircled by it and entry to the CBD was well nigh impossible. I was desolated. I could see our congregation

167

going down by half—and the 'Thank You Lord' offering with it. 'We could lose tens of thousands of dollars,' I complained to my wife. 'This is a disaster.'

Somehow I managed to sleep fairly well, but when I woke that Sunday morning, I was not my usual buoyant self. I love Sunday mornings. I look forward to being at church. Our services are exciting and inspiring. People are warm and friendly. We have a strong pastoral team who work together cheerfully and well. There is a great group of young people and young adults. The singing, the fellowship, the spirit of faith and joy, the brotherly love, the involvement—these are all inspirational. I always finish the day weary but uplifted. But on this occasion I was tense and concerned.

Because of the inevitable traffic congestion, we thought of taking the train, but we had invited folks home for lunch and needed the car as they had no transport. So we left early and hoped we would find a way through. All the way as we were driving, we thought and talked about the situation.

At that time, there were huge problems with the American economy—two of the nation's largest mortgage financiers were in trouble and some banks had been forced to close. The ripples were being felt in Australia as well and there was growing alarm about housing, employment and superannuation. There was no doubt some people would be experiencing increasing financial stress. This was an added concern.

In my preoccupation with these questions, I missed the exit

from the motorway and had to detour across the Harbour and back again, which added nearly half an hour to our travel time. This was not a calming experience. Finally, we managed to get within three blocks of the Mission and decided to walk the rest.

I was to speak that morning on 'Overflowing with Thanksgiving'. Earlier I had asked Vanessa if she could think of a good story I could use of someone who had rejoiced in time of trouble. But somehow, in my concern about the offering, I forgot to follow this through. During the pre-service prayer meeting I recalled my need for a story. Suddenly, I realised that I knew someone that very day who needed to give thanks in adverse circumstances—me! So while others were praying about the gathering, I prayed over and over, 'Thank you, Lord, for a great offering today! I'm trusting you for an exceptional offering!' My fists were clenched and I was lifting my feet up and down, geeing myself up like an underdog before a tennis final. The more I rejoiced in the Lord, the stronger was my conviction that we just had to go ahead in faith.

When I walked into the theatre, the view was not encouraging, to say the least. There were empty seats everywhere. Basically, those who had come by public transport were present and that was about it. Gradually people began to dribble in. They were still entering the theatre an hour after we commenced! But it was obvious our overall attendance was down. I learned afterwards that many people had been stuck in traffic for an hour or more and that some had simply turned around and gone home.

I told the people the story of my own discouragement as honestly as I could. And I also shared with them how I felt God had convicted me that whether there were one hundred or one thousand people present, it made no difference. As long as he was with us, all would be well.

Our practice on 'Thank You Lord Sunday' was to have our regular offering at the usual time and then, after the message, to present the special offering. There would be ushers holding large baskets at the front of the theatre and, while we sang, the people would bring their gifts to the front and place them in the baskets. It was always an exciting and celebratory time.

And here again, things went wrong. I had asked the song leader to choose a familiar song that people could sing without needing to look at the screen while they came down the steps in the aisles to the front of the theatre. But somehow or other, he decided to choose a new song that we had never sung before. Arghh, another aggravation.

So when the time came, I asked people to listen to the new song and then, when I gave the signal, to bring their gifts. But they did not want to wait another moment—they just came anyway. They surged to the front. In my flustered state I tried to stop them, standing with my hands up like a traffic policeman. I had no more success than old King Canute who tried to stop the waves of the sea.

So I gave in and just watched the people come. Somehow, this foolish incident upset me further as I realised I had acted needlessly and left some people confused. One woman in particular was obviously annoyed at the misunderstanding, and glared at me with frustration. Although I knew her to be easily angered, the incident took the edge off the celebration.

Later I realised that I should have been grateful that the people were so eager to give. How many pastors would give almost anything to see their people thronging like this to bring their gifts to God.

Well, the service came to an end and the people gathered in the foyer as usual over their cuppa and their conversation. Some time later, one of the ushers manoeuvred his way through the crowd, approached me and asked, 'Would you like to know the total?'

'Of course,' I responded.

'Have a guess.'

'You tell me.'

'One hundred and fourteen thousand dollars!' he said with a smile.

I couldn't believe it. 'You're joking,' I said.

'Oh you of little faith,' he responded, chiding me for my unbelief.

'How much was it?' I asked again.

He told me again and I continued, 'That's unbelievable.'

He said, 'I've never seen so much money on the counting table in all the years I've been here.'

'Unbelievable,' I repeated.

I realised that there would be many people who had missed the service who would give more the following Sunday. It would be a remarkable offering for our congregation. The final total turned out to be over $136,000.

The next week, when I announced the figure that had been given, people clapped and cheered and praised the Lord. They were delighted at what the Lord had done through them.

I have no idea who won the Sydney Marathon that year. But I knew there was a whole congregation of people inside Wesley Theatre who had run a marathon of a different kind—and they were all winners.

A Woman's Woman

Dave Andrews

~

Caroline Chisholm was born into a wealthy rural English family in 1808. The Joneses were evangelical Christians. Her father brought his daughter up to stand by what she believed in, and her mother brought her daughter up to serve the poor.

So the fun-loving young Caroline grew up with a serious faith, a strong mind and a social conscience.

Caroline's father died when she was young, and her erstwhile wealthy family was suddenly plunged into desperate poverty. It was one thing for her to care for the poor; it was another thing for her to *be* poor herself. It was an experience Caroline never forgot.

When she reached a marriageable age, Caroline met Archibald Chisholm. He was an English officer in the Indian Army. He cut a dashing figure in his uniform, and when she got the chance to talk with him, Caroline found Archy had substance as well as style. So they decided to get married.

The Chisholms' marriage was anything but traditional. They decided it would be 'an equal partnership', as opposed to the 'superior–subordinate relationships' that were more common at the time. And though Caroline, who was Protestant, agreed to become Catholic like Archy, she only agreed on the proviso that she would be free to pursue any nondenominational philanthropic work that she felt called to—'without impediment'.

After their wedding Archy was recalled to India, and Caroline was to follow him later to Madras. Upon her arrival the officers' wives drew her into their party circuit—but Caroline loathed the petty gossip that filled the empty lives of the *burri memsahibs*.

Caroline's eye was caught more by the poverty than it was by the opulence. And she immediately began to pray that God would show her a way to respond to the plight of the hapless child prostitutes that swarmed around the outskirts of the garrison town.

Caroline eventually decided that the only way she could save the poor kids from prostitution—or marriages so degrading they were almost as bad—was to start a school that could teach them marketable skills.

The officers—and their wives—were scandalised by Caroline's 'unbecoming' behaviour, and they told Archy to pull his wife into line or risk becoming a 'social outcast'. But Archy refused to be bullied, throwing his lot in with the 'social outcasts' by personally underwriting the expenses of the school himself.

So with Archy's support, Caroline set up a modern school in Madras—teaching street kids not only reading and writing but also cooking and cleaning, budgeting and bookkeeping, and even nursing.

Some years later, due to ill health, Archy and Caroline applied to take long leave in Australia. They arrived in Sydney with their two children in 1838 and settled into a comfortable house in Windsor.

After a couple of years Archy had to go back to his regiment, but they decided it was best for Caroline and the children to stay on at their new home in New South Wales.

Caroline thought she might open a school in Sydney like she had in Madras. But as she prayed about it, she became convinced she needed to set the idea of a school aside for a while and get involved with the poor immigrant women—penniless widows and orphaned girls—who slept in tents in the Domain or in the streets around The Rocks.

Many of the women that Caroline met told tragic tales of fleeing destitution in England by emigrating to Australia, only to fall into the hands of abusive crews on board the ships, and unscrupulous brothel owners once the vessels docked in Sydney Harbour.

Upon hearing these stories, Caroline made it her business to meet every ship as it came in. To start with she took the women into her own home at Windsor. Then, when there were too many, she persuaded the wife of Governor Gipps to get her husband to make the old barracks on Bent Street available to her. She turned the rat-infested shed into an emergency shelter accommodating more than one hundred women at a time

Caroline then accompanied the residents around town in their search for work. When she couldn't find enough jobs around Sydney, she set up voluntary committees all around New South Wales to act as employment agencies for her. And she personally took her charges from Moreton Bay to Port Macquarie to secure proper employment for them.

In the process, Caroline secured employment for over fourteen thousand women. And to protect the rights of these women, Caroline introduced employment contracts, in triplicate, to ensure the provision of good basic conditions in their places of employment.

When Archy returned in 1845, Caroline talked to him about the need to take her campaign to Britain in order to lobby the British Government directly. So Archy agreed to return with her to England to take the fight for the rights of migrants to their point of origin.

Back in England Caroline met with the Secretary of State, the Home Secretary and the Land and Emigration Commissioners, providing them with detailed reports on human rights abuses and presenting them with specific policy options which they could adopt to address these issues.

While waiting for these reforms to be adopted, Caroline went ahead and organised a society to aid migrants, independent of, but in cooperation with, the British Government. The central committee of the society she organised, under the high-profile presidency of Lord Ashley MP (the Earl of Shaftesbury), with the public support of Charles Dickens, set up a scheme to help poor migrants with everything from safe travel to personal loans.

Caroline did all she could to expedite family reunions for ex-convicts, who were separated from their wives and children for years. She lobbied for free passage for these reunions, and for land reform to enable these families to get small farms of their own.

In 1854 Caroline joined Archy in Melbourne, where, since 1851, he had been running the Aussie end of their operation. Back in Australia Caroline continued her relentless campaign through the press and the parliament for women's entitlements.

By 1866 the Chisholms had exhausted their considerable intellectual, emotional and physical resources. They had worked passionately, without pay, in the service of humanity for more than a quarter of a century. And when they retired to England they were worn out. In 1877 Caroline died, and her beloved Archy died a few months later.

Caroline once said, 'I am not one of those who like to ask, "What will the government do for us?" The question of the day is, "What shall we do for ourselves?" ' Her life embodied the words of Jesus: 'As long as it is day, we must do the work of him who sent me. Night is coming, when no one can work' (John 9:4).

Where Are All the People?

Christine Caine

'Where are all the people?' I asked Nick. The look he gave me as an answer to my question made me laugh, because it was the same expression he frequently gives to Catherine when she asks him an absurd question. And I guess I could understand his surprise at my words—after all, we were standing in a crowd of hundreds of tourists in one of the most majestic European churches ever constructed. But a lack of people wasn't what I meant.

'No, I mean the church. Where is the church?' I said. And there again, staring back at me, was Nick with that look.

'Chris, what are you talking about? We're standing right inside of it,' he replied.

'No, I mean the people *in* the church.' Before he got another word in, I started to explain myself. 'What we're standing in right now isn't the church; it's just a building. And I realise that we are in a crowd of hundreds, but where are all of the people who once made this building a church? When

179

did this stop being a place where people gathered to worship God and instead became an empty building that people pay money to visit?'

Nick finally got it, and his expression changed. As he opened his mouth, ready to respond, I beat him to the punch (what can I say, I was on a roll).

'I mean, think about it. It must have taken decades to build this structure, let alone create all the amazing murals and carvings. Many of the men who were part of this building project probably didn't even live to see the finished product or attend one of the worship services. And look at all the intricate details of every single square inch of this place, all to give glory to God. Not to mention the cost! It must have taken some passion to make this all come to pass. What would these people think if they could see that their house of God was now nothing more than a tourist attraction? They would be devastated.' (Yes, Nick, like you, often wonders if I ever stop to take a breath.)

Nick and I looked around again, suddenly seeing this amazing building with very different eyes. As the builders laboured to finish this magnificent house of God, I imagine the thing that kept them going was a vision of the lives that would be transformed as a result of their tireless efforts. They would have thought about the countless souls who would encounter God in that building, the bodies that would be healed, the marriages restored, the life-giving sermons preached, the prayers prayed, the ministries birthed, the friendships formed and the incredible worship to God that would take place.

As the builders faithfully laid each stone, their purpose was never about the bricks and mortar but about the people who would be impacted and changed once the cement had set. It's true that the actual building was fashioned to be grand and breathtaking, but this was because these men wanted to inspire people by using this building as a reflection, a glimpse, of the excellence and majesty of God. The architecture was not the goal in and of itself—it was only a means to an end. The purpose of the ornate building was to attract people to God (not to the building).

Yet today, Nick and I were standing among hundreds of people waiting patiently to take photos of the building—the bricks and mortar. As they clicked away with their cameras, their comments to one another suggested that they thought they were taking pictures of the church. But the reality was that the church—that is, the people of God—had left this building long ago, and in their place were the empty pews and beautiful artwork. We could no longer see evidence of the power and life of God's Spirit working in his people, just a building that once housed the church.

Sadly this experience is one that I have frequently encountered as I minister in many different cities around the world, and it is the exact opposite of what God designed the church to be. In the second commandment, Jesus said that we are to love our neighbour as we love ourselves. As the church, we are called to love our neighbourhood and the diverse people represented in it. This is difficult to do if the church has left the building!

The word 'church' comes from the Greek word *ecclesia*, which is defined as 'an assembly' or 'called out ones'. The root meaning of 'church' doesn't pertain to a building but rather to a people. That's you and me!

Two Men Walk into an Inn...

Michael Frost and Alan Hirsch

⸎

Two middle-aged men meet in an inn in a small, unremarkable village. They embrace, their heavy, solid hands slapping each other's broad backs affectionately. They kiss twice, on each cheek. They sit and eat, hunching over the shared table in a conspiratorial way. The dust that coats their faces highlights the deepening lines around their eyes. Their greying beards betray the years. They are like two old lions, warriors who've fought many a battle but live to fight another day.

Wiping crumbs from his moustache with the back of his hand, one says with a smirk, 'You've gotten old quickly.'

The other looks up and raises his eyebrows.

'I just mean,' continues the first man, 'I haven't seen you for a while, and you seem to have aged quite a bit in that time.' Another smirk.

The other man starts to defend himself but instead waves his hand dismissively at his friend. 'Why do I even bite at comments like that?' he smiles. 'You're not exactly the strapping young fellow you used to be either, you know.'

They both smile, and the first man reaches across and places his hand on his friend's arm. The tone turns serious. 'It's the travel that wears me out,' he confesses.

'Agreed. And the disappointment. I could bear the travel, the strange lodgings, the mishaps. But the disappointment of hearing about comrades turning from the cause or cells diverting from our doctrine, well, that's what wears me out the most. I've heard it makes me look old,' he says, eyeing his friend warily.

'Very old, actually.' They laugh. Silence.

After a while, the first man says, 'The Corinthians still causing you a headache, Paul? Should I blame them for all your grey whiskers?'

'Headaches and whiskers are nothing, Peter. Have you heard the latest? You don't want to know. Jealousy, quarrels and divisions. Some of them have even rejected me as an apostle. Apparently, they prefer more gifted leaders! Can you believe that? They don't understand that wisdom is from the Spirit. After even such a long time, they're still babies in Christ. Don't get me started on their list of crimes: sexual immorality, lawsuits among the comrades, abuse of freedom, tolerance of immoral brothers, taking pride in their spiritual gifts, chaotic and disorderly worship, improper theology on resurrection, and, well, just a complete lack of love. I've written them four letters about all this, and each one seems to get me into further trouble with them. I'm of a mind to stop writing and start fighting. Teach 'em a lesson with my fists that my letters obviously can't. Actually you're probably a better fighter than me. Fancy a trip to Corinth?'

'Clobbering Corinthians probably won't do the trick, comrade. Though I *am* inclined to join you,' Peter smiles sympathetically.

'How is the cell at Galatia? Have you had contact with them?' Paul asks after downing a mouthful from his cup. Peter shakes his head slowly. Paul continues, 'Their faith was not strong enough to resist the confusions stirred up by the teaching of the Jewish Christians about the circumcision requirement, and they doubted the gospel I preached to them. Like the Corinthians, they even doubt my authority, too.'

And so it goes. Two tired men sharing back and forth, recounting stories of new cells in Asia Minor, new converts in Europe, new developments in Greece.

Finally Paul says, 'Peter, I'm not sure when I'll see you again ...'

'You say that every time we get together.'

'I know, and it's always true. But in case our paths never cross again, can you tell me about him one more time.'

Peter smiles sadly, 'Oh, Paul, you've heard me tell you those stories a million times. You tell them yourself better than I do.'

Paul leans forward toward his friend. 'Comrade, I've been

beaten, abandoned, betrayed, shipwrecked and left for dead. It's hard to think of a cell I've planted that isn't in the grip of some crisis, personal or doctrinal. I'm not well. I'm often hungry. And, well, according to some of my friends, I look like an old man. The revolution is unfolding, slowly but surely. Ah, the things we've seen. But at times it feels arduous. I long for the Lord as the watchman longs for the end of night. And there are times when I wonder whether these small, struggling cells we're planting will become the movement we dreamed of. Yes, I do wonder. Even after all I've seen and done. All *we've* seen and done . . .'

Then he fixes his eyes firmly on Peter's and says, pleading, 'Tell me again.'

We can imagine ourselves standing in the doorway of the ancient inn, looking into the darkened room and seeing two battle-weary warriors sharing stories of their hero, their standard, their inspiration. Would Paul and Peter have met like this and spoken in this way? Who can say? But there seems little doubt that it was the story of Jesus that inspired their work and ministry and was the lifeblood of their mission.

Indeed, writing to the Romans, Paul introduces himself as 'Paul, a servant of Christ Jesus, called to be an apostle, set apart for the gospel of God' (Rom 1:1). What is the 'gospel of God' for which he felt set apart? Is it a set of doctrinal propositions, a revolutionary dogma, a collection of beliefs and practices centred on Jesus? In fact, it's far more. The gospel is not simply theological ideology. It is a historical event! Listen as he explains:

> *[the gospel] he promised beforehand through his prophets in the holy scriptures, the gospel concerning his Son, who was descended from David according to the flesh and was declared to be Son of God with power according to the spirit of holiness by resurrection from the dead, Jesus Christ our Lord, through whom we have received grace and apostleship to bring about the obedience of faith among all the Gentiles for the sake of his name, including yourselves who are called to belong to Jesus Christ. (Romans 1:2–6)*

When Paul explains the content of his gospel, it doesn't consist of propositional statements about creation, sin, atonement and redemption. It is a recapturing of the historical story of Jesus! For Paul, the gospel *is* Jesus—his messianic credentials, his physical descent from David, his vindication by the Spirit of God, and his resurrection from the dead. This looks identical to the gospel given to us in Matthew's Gospel. In effect, Romans 1:1–6 is a *Reader's Digest* version of the Gospels.

Bible quotations are from the New Revised Standard Version.

Miracle on the Mountain

Charles Widdowson

here were four of us on the trip to the Philippines: Alice and myself, with our second daughter, Judith, and our friend Ian, a youth pastor from Broadmeadows in Melbourne. I had told them all about my previous trip [see 'Three Lessons in Humility', pp. 136–144] and all four of us were excited at the prospect of being a part of my Shangri-La.

The plan was to travel to Baguio City, where we had been invited to minister for a couple of days, and then go on to Kapangan in the mountains.

But it was hot! Evidently we'd arrived during a time of prolonged dry weather with little chance of a let-up for weeks to come. We hadn't taken *that* into account! It meant that water was becoming scarce and ruled out any possibility of a cool shower or bath.

'Do you want to come to Kapangan, sweetheart?' I asked Alice as we tried to keep cool in our Baguio City hotel. 'Or would you rather stay here where there's at least *some* water and you *can* get a cup of tea?'

'We promised to go and, what's more important, we really believe that Father wants us to go. We're only going to be there a couple of days and I'm sure I'll manage somehow.' She paused. 'The only thing I am concerned about is the "bus" trip.'

Even though I'd tried to convince Alice that the trip from Baguio City to Kapangan really wasn't all that bad, she had remembered my vivid description after my first visit.

'Darling,' I tried to encourage her, 'forget the journey. Believe me, it will be well worth it. I'll be sitting next to you, and once you meet Gavino and all the people, you'll be absolutely thrilled. In any case, the air could well be clearer and fresher up there—and cooler,' I added.

To try to distract ourselves from the thought of riding in the 'bus', we had lunch at the Peak Hotel in Baguio and then made our way to the Dangwar Terminal.

The 'bus' was there, and to my surprise seemed slightly more comfortable than last time and not quite as crowded. The road, however, hadn't improved one bit!

Slowly the 'bus' jolted along and we all bumped up and down with every jolt. But the air didn't become cooler, and dust and flies were coming in through the open windows. There was, of course, no air conditioning.

As we drew near to the mission compound we were to visit, we heard the bell announcing our arrival. I looked at my watch.

Praise God, the journey had taken two instead of three hours. It was now four o'clock.

Oh! how good it was to see Gavino and all the folk again. There was much hugging and laughter as sticky body was wrapped around equally sticky body. I introduced Alice, Judith and Ian to Gavino and he graciously welcomed us all.

Then nearby we heard something that is virtually impossible to describe: the crystal clear voices of Kapangan children singing praises to God.

We turned and looked. A young girl, no older than seven, was the 'choir mistress', and under her direction pure harmony was filling the whole campus. All we could do was to stand in awe of such innocent worship.

As soon as they had finished, all the children came rushing towards us, hugging us and putting their little faces up to be kissed.

'Yes,' Alice whispered to me while still being hugged, 'this is heaven.'

It was only then, as we began to walk across to Gavino's house, that we noticed all the other people who were there. In ones, twos and families there must have been fifty or more of them, carrying jugs, mugs or tins carefully across the campus.

'What are they doing?' Alice asked me.

Gavino overheard and answered her. 'Look up and see how clear the sky is. It's been like this for weeks. None of us have very much water, but we all know that you are from Australia, and Charles told us that you like your cup of tea, Alice. So out of their small supply, each one has walked miles to bring an offering of water. All four of you beautiful people will be able to wash, shave *and* have your cups of tea.'

Suddenly, as we stood there totally overwhelmed by the sacrifice that was being made, it happened. A cloud appeared in the clear, blue sky and it began to rain. For about ten minutes sweet, refreshing, life-giving rain poured from above. Then, as suddenly as it had started, it ceased. The cloud disappeared, the searing heat returned, and within minutes the ground had dried and it was as if nothing had taken place.

'You know,' Gavino said, 'that amount of rain would have refilled every dam and tank in the area.'

We had a praise service on the spot, and that night's meeting was unlike any other that the four of us had ever been a part of. Our God is the God of the miraculous!

A Box of Chocolates

Anusha Atukorala

~

I'd been browsing for a while. In one hand was a large green bag which contained several other green bags. They were for my grocery shopping later. Right now, though, I was focused on gifts I needed to purchase. I chose four items. Then I made my way to the checkout counter of the department store.

Oh! I realised with dismay that I had one item too many to pass through the three-items-or-less express checkout.

Never mind! I wasn't in a big hurry, was I? I queued behind others, dropping items clumsily as I tried to balance them all. *There, that's better,* I thought to myself as I picked up a fallen shirt and hastily grabbed at the book that was on the verge of following suit.

When it was my turn at the checkout, I scratched my head in puzzlement. *Hmmm,* I thought. I'd had four items but now I only had three. *I wonder what happened to the other one?* There wasn't time to worry about that. I quickly handed the shirt, the book and the pair of socks I had in my hands to the smiling girl at the checkout. I paid for the purchases and made my way out of the store.

Minutes later, I was at the post box at the other end of the shopping centre. I was about to pop my snail mail letters and cards into the post box when I started in surprise.

What was that box of chocolates doing inside my green bag?

It took me a few seconds to realise that the box of chocolates was the fourth item I'd meant to buy in the shop. It must have slipped down into the bag while I'd been doing that balancing act with the other gifts. I couldn't believe my eyes. But yes, there was no mistaking it. There it was—a large box of chocolates, gazing up at me. And I hadn't paid for it.

There was, of course, only one thing to be done. I hurriedly walked the length of the shopping centre, in the opposite direction this time. I reached the store. I went inside. I rushed to the checkout. I paid for the item. I'd almost been holding my breath, wondering if there would be a problem. Thankfully there wasn't and all went well.

I breathed a sigh of relief as I walked out of the shop. It seemed that for a little while I'd been a shoplifter. Me? A shop lifter? Oh no!

True, my mistake wasn't intentional. But what a terrible discovery! If the alarm had sounded as I was I leaving the shop earlier, what might have happened?

Mistakes! We all make them. Some are small, others not so

small. This blunder was a big one. What a good thing it didn't blow up into an embarrassing incident. This error was fairly easy to rectify, but there are other mistakes that are not as easy to undo.

If someone else had been caught shoplifting, what would I have thought? Would I have given her the benefit of the doubt, or would I have wondered why she had done it? Do I judge others without knowing all the facts behind their actions? I am ashamed to admit I probably do.

I was reminded of a verse I'd recently read in scripture: 'Do not judge others or you too will be judged' (Matthew 7:1). That day, I realised that God expects me to mete out the same judgment that I would like others to extend towards me. Innocent until proven guilty!

If I don't want others to judge my actions or my mistakes, dare I judge another?

Making the Most of Each Day

John Mallison

❧

ost of us have heard the quote many times: 'Live each day as if it were your last.' It seeks to remind us how our time is limited, how precious life is. It encourages us to seek to get our priorities right.

While serving in my denomination's State Board of Christian Education, I left home one evening to drive to the central west of our state for a very busy week of leadership-equipping events, commencing the next day in the rural city of Parkes.

It was a cold evening so I had all the windows of my car closed, and to dull the boredom of the long drive and in the hope of some inspiration I had my music CDs playing.

As I approached my destination, the road wound down a long hill then flattened out onto a level tract of country. Not having noticed any previous roadside warning signs, I was aghast to see right in front of me a railway level crossing and a freight train about to cross the road! I slammed on the brakes, but the lead engine tore the front off my car and spun me sideways so the many laden freight carriages sped past within centimetres of my near-side door.

I was unhurt, but being traumatised I was unable to move. The long train eventually stopped, and after some time the deeply shocked drivers of the train made their way back to the crash site. They were greatly relieved to find me unhurt and went on to explain that they had seen me winding down the hill and, concerned that I may not have seen the warning sign nor their headlight, had sounded their horn repeatedly. However, because I had the music playing and the car windows closed, I was totally unaware of their efforts to get my attention.

Eventually I was towed into the town, and after a very restless night I conducted a full day's conference the next day, which was surprisingly successful. However, without my car to transport all the resources for the following events in other towns, and realising I needed space to recuperate, I cancelled the rest of the week's schedule, left my unrepairable wrecked car and returned home by air.

Facing death, as I did in the above incident, certainly gave me a new perspective on life. However, I regret that all too often I forget that each day could be my last here on earth. I may not specifically ask myself each day, 'If today is my last day what should I do differently?' However, I seek to live each day responsibly—trying to use my time wisely and taking time to consider the big choices.

This seems to happen naturally during my morning times

of solitude in prayer and studying God's Word in which I thank God for his boundless love, amazing kindness and mercy. In these times I review my day's program and pray for others. As I do, frequently I am prompted to communicate my gratitude, encouragement, support and concern for others by making a phone call, writing a note, sending an email or arranging to meet a person. I note any such 'nudges', and over the years I have learnt to daily act promptly on them. I get sufficient positive feedback to convince me that it is God's Spirit who guides me.

As a Christ-follower I seek to take seriously the teachings of Jesus, so I would hope that no day ends without my attempting to obey his clear command to love as he loved. I seek to show Christ's love to others in various ways, some of which I have listed above. I frequently tell those who are closest to me how much I love them and why. I truly believe that being channels of God's love is what really matters. It should be the distinguishing mark of a disciple of Jesus Christ.

I thank God for the excellent health and remarkable opportunities to serve him that he has given me, all of which could have come to an abrupt end nearly thirty years ago!

Hope and Tears in the City of Smiles

Sheridan Voysey

~

ope and tears in the City of Smiles. That's how I'll remember the afternoon of Saturday 6 January 2007. On that afternoon a fifteen-year-old girl named Riza Gallego stole my heart, and then broke it. I've never been quite the same since.

It happened in the Philippines, where Merryn and I have two sponsor children. On this trip we'd meet both in person. We were excited and apprehensive all at once.

We flew to the island of Negros, arriving in the capital, Bacolod City—nicknamed the 'City of Smiles'—where we were to meet Riza. We had sponsored Riza for eight years, and during the last couple of those years her letters had become more and more personal. We had developed a bond.

We arrived at the simple restaurant where we were to meet, and took our seats. A moment later Riza walked in. Riza saw us and burst into tears. We saw Riza and fell in love.

Riza wore an apricot T-shirt with white ribbing, simply cut

jeans and sandals—the best of the few clothes she owned. We sat down to eat, with her sponsor agency workers. I'll never forget how Riza replied when asked what she'd like to drink. 'You mean, I can have *anything* on the menu?' Her eyes were wide and incredulous. Riza doesn't normally eat in restaurants. She ordered a mango smoothie—a rare treat.

Conversation began to flow once the emotions of our initial meeting subsided. We reviewed the basics. Riza's father is a welder, her mother a homemaker. Their house is a one-room shack shared with two dogs and a cat. At night Riza sleeps on the bed with her mother and her father sleeps on the 'couch' (no doubt more bamboo than cushion in construction). The electricity in her home powers one light bulb and a radio, and her wardrobe consists of a cardboard box in the corner of the room holding her school clothes. Riza and her family live simply. They have no other choice. That's why she needs sponsorship.

After lunch we drove to Mambukal Resort—a simple but popular Negros attraction with pools, forest walks and hot springs. I'd occasionally look at Riza as we walked along with our tour guide, wondering what her life might become. Riza wants to be a nurse when she leaves school. Will she succeed? How will she pay her college fees? Suddenly I wanted to kidnap her and bring her home. I wanted to be there at her graduation and at her wedding. I wanted to make sure she never wanted for anything again.

Darkness fell and we started the hour-long drive back to Bacolod City. It had been a magical day, and it was about to end.

'When are you going back Australia?' Riza asked me during the ride. I sombrely replied that we'd be off to Jakarta next, then home in a couple of days. 'Maybe we'll see each other again one day,' she said, and started to cry. Tears welled up in my eyes too. I couldn't promise that we'd ever see each other again, and I hated it.

We pulled into our motel's parking lot and got out of the van. Merryn and I turned to face Riza. She hugged us and began to walk away. After a few steps she ran back and hugged us again. I've never wept so much.

On Saturday 6 January 2007, I found a girl any parent would be proud of. Riza was polite, caring and had an innocence too rarely seen. You see, Riza's meagre living conditions mean she doesn't have the distractions we do. She's not sullied by materialistic desires. Riza's joy is in animals and flowers and natural wonders. Riza has nothing materially speaking but instead has a love for God and his world that would touch any atheist. 'Blessed are the poor,' Jesus said, 'for theirs is the kingdom of God.' I saw that in Riza.

Yes, there were tears in the City of Smiles that day. We're going to miss Riza terribly. But there was hope too. The few dollars we send each month has given Riza a future. And one day we'll see her again—in that place where every tear will turn to joy.

The Da Vinci Decision

Charles Fivaz

∽

I know Dan Brown's *The Da Vinci Code* is not so topical now. But then, you haven't heard *my* story about it. And you haven't heard what the Lord himself, the Author of authors, had to say about that controversial book.

It happened a few years ago when *The Da Vinci Code* was racing to the top of the bestseller lists around the world. In the months that followed, there appeared a plethora of reactionary books and articles by Christian writers debunking the blasphemous 'facts' in Brown's novel—books with titles like *Breaking the Da Vinci Code*, *The Gospel Code* and *Da Vinci Code Decoded*. But my story preceded them all, pipped them at the post, and if it had been published straight away, they may even have quoted me, I reckon.

I was on a Melbourne train bound for home after a taxing last day at the office, and I was wondering what reading matter I should take with me on my approaching holiday, when I overheard two fellow-passengers discussing their choice of current reading.

'Can't put it down,' said one. 'It's a real page-turner. Every chapter ends in a cliff-hanger.'

'What's it about?' enquired the other.

'*The Da Vinci Code*? Well, it's a murder mystery. And the investigation uncovers some truths that threaten to shake the foundations of Christianity.'

'Mmm. Sounds a bit iffy,' said the other. 'Religion?'

'Yeah, it's about the church hiding the true facts about Jesus, and going to murderous lengths to do so. It's a ripper of a book.'

Gripping novel. Murder mystery. Religious controversy. That got my interest going. Our flight to Maroochydore was departing the following day. *I suppose they have it at Melbourne airport*, I thought. Then an after-thought: *Must take a bit of serious spiritual reading too*. I already had a few books in the latter category piled up on the 'unread' shelf at home, just waiting for that longed-for holiday break. I'll take the Philip Yancey, I decided.

As the plane took off I felt a wave of pleasure at the thought of leaving behind the stressful demands of a working life, and a city in the grip of a prolonged drought. Gazing down at the brown landscape below as the plane angled its way up and out of a dried-up old Victoria, I remembered the many weeks of Tuesday nights my wife and I had sacrificed to attend a series of GreenHome seminars. It was our little effort to beat the effects of the drought, and save the planet too while we were about it. We could take a holiday break from all of that now as well, I thought—no more showering with a bucket, diverting the grey water into the garden and flushing the loo only when the contents were 'brown' (oh, how we winced at that idea at first!). None of that would be necessary in our little coastal paradise just a couple of hours away.

As we settled into the flight, I read the back cover of *The Da Vinci Code*, furtively, as I wasn't ready to discuss my reading choice with my wife just yet. Then I snuck it away for a later, more indulgent read. They said it would shake the foundations of Christianity, I mused in silence. But it *is* fiction, I argued internally, seeking to reassure my doubting self. I'm simply going to read the novel for what it is: pure fiction. I have an open mind. And I do need a bit of good fiction. That settled, I was at peace with my decision.

The Noosa unit was exactly what we'd hoped for: a quiet retreat with filtered bay views. Below the bedroom balcony you could see the tranquil blue through the lush garden that was thriving without the need of our grey water.

I revelled in the idea that there was actually nothing to do. My wife was out on the balcony basking in the sun. I was sitting on the edge of the bed with my two books, one in each hand, wondering which I should dive into first. In one hand I held Dan Brown and in the other I held Philip Yancey.

It was then that I remembered that I had not checked my choice of reading with the Lord—I had not put it to prayer, as

I do with most choices in life, even the small ones. So I prayed there and then: 'Lord, I've brought these two books along for relaxation and renewal. I'm sorry I did not put this to you more specifically before. But I do get the sense that you are okay with my choice. So please show me now if this is a good choice. And please show me which I should read first.'

At that point I held the two books up and waited, not knowing what to do next. Directly opposite me was the open door to the en suite. Then, for some reason, I stood up.

What happened next is not that clear. I'm not sure whether I stumbled or just lost my balance, but my body did a kind of momentary lurch. In the flurry to steady myself, my left hand let go its grip and the book it was clutching was released and began to travel through the air. I watched it, incredulously, fly through the open en suite door. I saw it in slow motion, twirling through the air and heading, unimpeded, for . . . the toilet.

It literally fell, without touching the sides, directly into the open toilet bowl. It landed in there with a spludge. Then silence.

The stillness was palpable. The silence was God's exclamation mark. And I was listening.

Then I called my wife in off the balcony. 'I want you to witness this,' I said, 'because no one's going to believe my story.'

She came in and peered into the bowl. Perplexed at the

sight of a half-sodden book rammed into the toilet, she asked, 'What book is that?'

'It's by Dan Brown,' I said. 'It's *The Da Vinci Code.*' Then I explained as best I could what had happened.

'What are you going to do with it?' she asked dreamily, struggling to work out an appropriate response.

I had an idea. 'What was that water-saving slogan they used at the GreenHome seminars last month?' I asked. 'The one about the toilet.'

She thought for a moment. 'If it's yellow let it mellow, if it's brown flush it down?'

'That's it!' I said, leaving a measured little pause before concluding, '. . . and as you can see, it *is* Brown!'

I Am with You

Margo Mangan

❧

I was out walking early one morning, just a couple of days after Christmas. I 'headed for the hills' where it was quiet and peaceful. I felt that I would much rather enjoy the bush than mix with the throngs of people crowding the shops in their search for the ultimate bargain.

After leaving suburbia behind and turning the first corner, I came across a shady patch of road, where the breeze was gentle and soothing against my skin, and I could smell the bush around me. It provided refreshment for the day ahead, which was expected to be hot.

A little further on there was a wisteria bush, a remnant left by someone who long ago had dumped their garden waste beside the road. It bore just four small sprigs of blossom. They looked beautiful—exquisite shades of purple, fragile and delicate—and three or four months later than wisteria bushes would usually bloom in our district. Its beauty touched me.

Around another corner the distant laughter of kookaburras

floated through the air, a sound created by a God who doesn't seem to take creation nearly as seriously as we sometimes do. When I hear kookaburras, it seems to me that God is sharing a joke with whoever chooses to listen.

After reaching the end of the road, I turned back towards home. The three-quarter moon caught my eye. It was high in the western sky and it shone amazingly brightly in the blue of the early morning sky.

Four things had caught my attention. None of them was of great importance by itself, but together they gave the same message from God that Jesus brought to the world so long ago. 'Emmanuel—I am with you. In the big things, in the little things, at every twist and turn of life, I am there!'

I don't know how many other love messages God placed along my path that morning, but I was so glad that I had noticed at least some of them. Are you open to receiving God's messages as they are revealed in the little things of life?

Contributors

Dave Andrews, his wife, Ange, and their family, have lived and worked with marginalised people in Australia, Afghanistan, Pakistan, India and Nepal for more than thirty years. They now live in a large joint household with their children, grandchildren and others in an inner-city community in Brisbane. The author of several books on radical spirituality and incarnational community, Dave is a part of the Waiters' Union, an inner city Christian community network working with Aborigines, refugees and people with disabilities, and an educator-at-large for TEAR Australia. <www.daveandrews.com.au>

Anusha Atukorala has two places she calls home: the beautiful island of Sri Lanka and what she calls 'this very special land Down Under'. Since she arrived in Adelaide eleven years ago, she has found her niche as an active member of the Golden Grove Baptist Church. She enjoys writing in any form, be it creative writing, composing songs and poetry, or simply emailing family and friends. Anusha lives in Adelaide with her husband Shan and their nineteen-year-old son, Asela.

Brad Baker is the Manager of Exhibition Development and Design at the Powerhouse Museum in Sydney. He has lectured in post-graduate design at the University of Technology, Sydney, and has worked for more than twenty years as a youth group leader in local churches. He is married to Kareena and they have six children.

Jane Beale was born on Kangaroo Island, off the coast of South Australia. In 2005 she developed her own business, 'Sign & Speak Australia', writing and teaching beginner level workshops for communicating with sign language. A senior speech pathologist, piano teacher and animal lover, Jane directs and performs with *The Singing Hands Choir* on the New South Wales Central Coast. The group has grown from six to twenty-six members in under three years, delighting audiences with their unique style of key word signing to inspirational music. Contact Jane at <singinghands@iinet.net.au>.

Amos Bennett worked for forty years as a journalist and broadcaster in the Central West of New South Wales, including twenty-five years as a news journalist and news editor with ABC Radio in Orange. On retirement 1998, Amos and his wife moved to Caloundra, on the Queensland Sunshine Coast, where he has spent the last six years serving in a voluntary capacity as media officer for Mercy Ships in Australia.

Nathan Brown is a writer and editor based in Warburton, Victoria. He has written for a wide variety of publications in Australia and around the world. His first novel, *Nemesis Train* (Ark House Press), was published in 2008 and he is in the midst of a number of other book projects. He is also a supporter of Opportunity International. <http://nemesistrain.blogspot.com>

Christine Caine describes herself as 'a pink Vespa-riding, world-travelling, Greek, Australian, wife, mum, author and preacher.' She is one of the pastors and directors of Equip & Empower Ministries, as well as the founder of The A21 Campaign to fight human trafficking. Based in

Sydney, she spends much of the year travelling with her husband Nick and daughters Catherine and Sophia 'to reach the lost, strengthen leadership, champion the cause of justice and build the local church globally'. <www. equipandempower.org>

Barry Chant is Senior Pastor of the Wesley International Congregation, part of Sydney's extensive Wesley Mission. He is an ordained minister in the CRC Churches International and was founding president of Tabor College. A best-selling author, speaker, theological educator and historian of the Pentecostal movement in Australia, he also likes to play tennis, cheer for the Sydney Swans AFL team and watch quality British television. He and his wife, Vanessa, have three adult children and twelve grandchildren.

Karl Faase is the senior pastor at Gymea Baptist Church, Sydney. He is the executive director of the Australian Arrow Leadership Development Program and founder and consultant with the 'Jesus. All about Life' media campaigns, which have run in Adelaide, Canberra, Tasmania and, in 2009, across New South Wales. Karl is also the director of 'Olive Tree Media', which produces radio and television programs, including the television special and DVD *Remembering '59* (2009). Karl's radio spots are heard on Christian stations across Australia, with a selection of them collected in the book *Just a Minute*. <www.olivetreemedia.com.au>

Charles Fivaz is a freelance writer who lives with his wife and three cats in an outer Melbourne suburb. Before settling in Australia in 1989, he lived and worked in South Africa, Holland, England and America. Apart from his passion for writing about spirituality, he has also been a programmer, singer-actor, amateur photographer (with exhibits in Cape Town's National Gallery) and Arts/Theology student.

Aussie Stories

Michael Frost is Professor of Evangelism and Missions at Morling College, Sydney, and is the missional architect of an innovative church in Manly called smallboatbigsea. He is the author of several books including *Exiles: Living Missionally in a Post-Christian World* (2006) and (with Alan Hirsch) *The Shaping of Things to Come* (2003) and *ReJesus* (2009). He travels extensively in the USA, Canada, the UK, Australia and New Zealand seeking to fan into flame the Western church's latent missional potential.

Az Hamilton moved from his hometown of Toowoomba to Brisbane in 2003 to take a job at Christian radio station *96five* as their night presenter. Along with AFL legend Shaun Hart, Commonwealth Games gold medallist Deb Lovely and the Brisbane Bronco's Brad Thorn, he was involved in 'Cool Choices', speaking in schools to inspire young people to live beyond themselves. After an April 2008 trip to Central America, he joined Compassion Australia as the organisation's youth communications specialist, with a heart to be a voice for children who can't speak up for themselves. <ahamilton@compassion.com.au>

Aaron Hardke and his wife Kellie have been involved with the Lutheran Church since they met as toddlers during their regular Sunday school lessons. They have worked in Queensland Lutheran schools for over ten years and both attended the Australian Lutheran World Service Teacher Study Tour to Nepal in 2007. Aaron is currently the Head of Learning and Teaching (P–9) at Redeemer Lutheran College in Rochedale, Brisbane.

Alan Hirsch is an author, missional strategist, cultural architect, speaker and leadership trainer. He is the founding director of Forge Mission Training Network and a founding director of the online learning forum Shapevine.

He is the author of several books including (with Michael Frost) *The Shaping of Things to Come* (2003) and *ReJesus* (2009). He and his wife Debra are currently based in Los Angeles where Alan is studying for a PhD at Fuller Theological Seminary. <www.shapevine.com/pg/blog/alanhirsch>

Grenville Kent is the besotted husband of Carla and the proud father of four young children. He lectures in Old Testament and Cultural Apologetics at Wesley Institute in Sydney, and travels internationally as an evangelical speaker, especially to students. Trained as a film-maker, Grenville is producing *Big Questions,* a documentary film series on the existence of God. He loves playing sports with his children and eats too much garlic.

John Mallison is a retired Uniting Church minister. As a Christian educator he has conducted leadership development events in twenty-nine countries and authored twenty-two books. He now devotes himself to caring for his wife, who has dementia. However, he continues to mentor a number of leaders as well as doing some writing and pastoring many in need. For his services to the community, he received the Order of Australia Medal. The Australian College of Theology awarded him an honorary Doctorate of Theology for his extensive publications and contribution to the church worldwide.

Margo Mangan is a wife, mum and grandma who lives in Tamworth. She is a lay preacher within the Uniting Church and is involved in the inter-denominational Emmaus community. She enjoys walking, photography, gardening and cooking. She is a volunteer pastoral visitor at a local nursing home, where she receives far more than she gives when she spends time with the residents.

Gordon Moyes has been a member of the New South Wales Legislative Council since 2003, first for the Christian Democratic Party and, since 2009, as an independent Christian politician. The superintendent for twenty-seven years of Wesley Mission, Sydney, he was made a Companion of the Order of Australia in 2002, Australia's highest honour. He has authored over fifty-nine books and booklets, scripted forty-six documentary films and hosted weekly radio and television programs. He produces a weekly e-magazine, 'A Christian Voice in Politics'. <www.gordonmoyes.com>

Adele Nash works as an editorial assistant at the Signs Publishing Company and edits *The Edge*, a bi-monthly magazine and website for young adults. She lives in Warburton, Vic., and loves the snow on Mt Donna Buang in winter. <www.edgeonweb.org>

Dorothy O'Neill is an author and freelance writer who has been published extensively in magazines in Australia, the UK and the USA. For ten years (1978–88) she was editor of *Encounter*, the magazine of ACTS (A Christian Teaching Service) International. The author of nine books, she now lives in a retirement home in Adelaide and attends a nearby Anglican church.

Paul O'Rourke is CEO of Compassion Australia. Prior to joining the child development organisation he had a long career as editor-in-chief of daily and suburban newspapers in both NSW and Queensland. He and his wife, Janine, have three children and two grandchildren, and they live in Newcastle, NSW.

Nola Passmore has taught psychology at the University of Southern Queensland in Toowoomba since 1989. She met her husband Tim through the Christian staff group there, and has a passion for applying the Christian worldview to the university setting. She is currently researching adoption issues, particularly with a view to helping those affected by adoption, and is pursuing her love of the creative arts via a Graduate Diploma in Creative Writing at Tabor Adelaide.

Kel Richards is an author, journalist and broadcaster. He currently works as a producer and presenter with the ABC's national NewsRadio network, and writes and presents the popular WordWatch radio program. The author of over forty books, he was awarded the degree of Master of Letters at the level of High Distinction by the University of New England for his thesis critiquing the writings of noted atheist Richard Dawkins.

Mandy Smith grew up in Australia but since 1989 has lived in the US and UK. She is a freelance writer and speaker and is Associate Pastor at University Christian Church in Cincinnati, USA. Her first book, *Life Is Too Important to be Taken Seriously: Kite-Flying Lessons from Ecclesiastes*, is available at <www.collegepress.com>.

Nicole Starling is married to Dave who lectures in New Testament and Theology at Morling College in Sydney. She has three children aged 7, 5 and 3. Before becoming a mum she studied arts/law and worked as an editor in a legal publishing company. Her personal blog is called *168 hours*, where she thinks out loud about what it means for her to follow Jesus in her everyday life; she also writes for *The Sola Panel* and coordinates the *EQUIP book club*. < http://168hrs.blogspot.com/>

Ian Stolz is a member of Resurrection Lutheran Church, Indooroopilly, Brisbane.

Irene Voysey was born and educated in India, and later lived in Hong Kong for seventeen years where she wrote a best-seller, *Houseplants for Asian*

Homes. She was editor of the Bible Society in Australia's magazine, *The Sower,* for ten years. She now lives on the New South Wales Central Coast and has recently enjoyed working with photographer Ken Duncan on two new books. She is presently copy-writing for Christian Action Asia and The Bible Society of Mongolia.

Sheridan Voysey is a Sydney-based writer, speaker and broadcaster. Author of the award-winning *Unseen Footprints: Encountering the Divine Along the Journey of Life* (Scripture Union, 2005) and *Open House: Sheridan Voysey in Conversation* (Strand Publishing, 2008), he contributes a regular column on spirituality and belief to *Alive Magazine* and is a feature writer for *Our Daily Journey*. He hosts *Open House*, a Sunday evening Australia-wide radio talkback show exploring life, faith and culture, and speaks at conferences and major events on the contemporary search for belief. <www.thethoughtfactory.net>

Scott Wegener is a graduate of the Melbourne School of Art and Photography and ran his own multimedia business for several years. He is currently web developer at Adventist Media Network in Wahroonga, NSW. He admits to looking on the lighter side of life's predicaments and encourages everyone to 'Be joyful always!'

Charles Widdowson, who turned eighty in June 2008, has been an ordained minister for over forty-five years. From 1975 to 1996 he and his wife, Alice, travelled world-wide in a preaching, teaching and training capacity. They are now 'Grandma and Grandpa', serving under Senior Pastors Rob and Christie Buckingham in Bayside Church, Cheltenham, Victoria. Charles also broadcasts on 89.9 Light FM, Melbourne. They have four children, ten grandchildren and two great-grandchildren.

Philip Yancey is a best-selling author whose books include *The Jesus I Never Knew*, *What's So Amazing about Grace?* and *Prayer: Does It Make Any Difference?*, all published by Zondervan. He is editor-at-large for *Christianity Today* magazine. <www.philipyancey.com>

Credits

'Looking Back' by Grenville Kent appeared in *Adventist Review*, 11 November 2004.

'The Climb', © 2009 Jane Beale.

'The Charlotte Rocker', © 2008 Gordon Moyes.

'The Bearded-Lady Jesus' by Michael Frost and Alan Hirsch is taken from their book *ReJesus: A Wild Messiah for a Missional Church* (Hendrickson Publishers/Strand Publishing, 2009), pp. 92–95.

'Smileys from God?' by Nicole Starling first appeared in her blog <http://168hrs.blogspot.com>.

'From the Ashes of Black Saturday' by Adele Nash is adapted from *Signs of the Times*, April 2009.

'The Difference a Night Can Make', © 2009 Karl Faase.

'How Long?', © 2009 Anusha Atukorala.

'In Their Shoes' by Aaron Hardke is adapted from *The Lutheran*, 12 November 2007. The original story won second place in the social justice category of the Australasian Religious Press Association (ARPA) awards for 2008.

'The Ever-Shrinking Keynote', © 2009 Nola Passmore.

'Seven Days, Seven Dollars' by Az Hamilton is adapted from the website of Compassion Australia <www.compassion.com.au>.

'Saved Letters', © 2009 Irene Voysey.

'A Man Who Embodied Jesus' by Michael Frost and Alan Hirsch is taken from their book *ReJesus: A Wild Messiah for a Missional Church* (Hendrickson Publishers/Strand Publishing, 2009), p. 66.

'Not Snail Mail, Not Email but . . .', © 2009 Anusha Atukorala.

'I Don't Know', © 2009, John Mallison.

'Mr Eternity' by Brad Baker is adapted from his paper 'Preserving Our Christian Heritage', in *Shaping the Good Society in Australia*, edited by Stuart Piggin (Australia's Christian Heritage National Forum, 2006), pp. 34–35.

'Life on the Flip Side', © 2009 Mandy Smith.

'The Great Exchange', © 2008 Sheridan Voysey, first appeared in *Alive Magazine*, August/September 2008.

'Air Rage' by Scott Wegener first appeared in *Signs of the Times*, July 2008.

'Floating Mercy' by Amos Bennett is adapted from the news website *Christian Today Australia* <http://au.christiantoday.com>.

'Three Lessons in Humility', © 2009 Charles Widdowson.

'Mexican Encounter', © 2009 Nola Passmore.

'Opportunity Maker' by Nathan Brown appeared in *Signs of the Times*, July 2008.

'The Miner's Lamp', © 2008 Gordon Moyes. Stuart Piggin's research on the Moonta revival has been published as 'Two Australian Spiritual Awakenings: Moonta Mines 1875 and Loddon River 1883', *Evangelical Review of Theology*, 31.1, January 2007, pp. 60–70.

You can contribute to Aussie Stories 2010

Do you have a story to tell that will move and inspire others? We believe that Australian Christians have a wealth of stories to tell—stories rooted in the rich, vibrant experience of following Jesus in this beautiful land. Stories that describe what people have seen and heard God do in their lives and the lives of others around them.

The *Aussie Stories* series, now in its eighth year, is dedicated to telling these stories. We welcome submissions of stories to be considered for inclusion in the next edition, due out in November 2010.

Submissions should be genuine stories—not sermons, Bible studies or devotional reflections. The length should be between 500 and 2500 words. Both unpublished and previously published material is welcome (if it has been published before, please include details).

Share your story with others and pass on God's goodness!

The Publishers

Email your stories, together with your contact details, to: strand@ bigpond.com